THE
ORIGINAL
SIN

JIM GOAD

OBNOXIOUS
BOOKS

Whiteness: The Original Sin

Published by Obnoxious Books, Stone Mountain, GA

ISBN-13: 978-1729700419
ISBN-10: 1729700411

To buy signed copies of Jim Goad's other books, visit www.jimgoad.net

Cover design by Sean Tejaratchi

Table of Contents

1

Whiteness: The Original Sin

According to the modern moral framework as it's dictated to us by academia's huddled rodents, the worst possible thing anyone can be is a racist. We are also increasingly lectured that all white people are racist—*so* racist, they don't even realize it, even when they're trying their best *not* to be racist. Therefore, it's not a giant leap to assume that under the current moral *Reich*, the worst possible thing anyone can be is a white person.

In Oklahoma—"one of the last places in America one might assume it's still at least somewhat OK rather than innately sinful to be white"—a minor scandal erupted when a high-school teacher was recorded on a smartphone camera ululating thusly to his students:

*Am I racist? And I say yeah. I don't want to be. It's not
like I choose to be racist, but do I do things because of the
way I was raised. To be white is to be racist, period.*

The teacher, James Coursey, made these comments
while showing a video in which a man applied
whiteout all over the globe to demonstrate the
allegedly pernicious effects of unbridled whiteness.
Coursey's lecture was recorded by a mixed-race
female student who told a reporter:

*Half of my family is Hispanic, so I just felt like, you know,
him calling me racist just because I'm white....I mean,
where's your proof in that? I felt like he was encouraging
people to kind of pick on people for being white. You start
telling someone something over and over again that's an
opinion, and they start taking it as fact.*

Much of the public, including all the gelded and
deluded "goodwhites," have swallowed such nonsense as fact simply because such propaganda is
relentlessly sprinkled through all levels of education these days like a cancer patient being seeded
with radiation pellets.

Early in 2016, an elite grade school on the Upper
West Side of Manhattan made headlines because it
segregated white and nonwhite students into sep-
arate study groups: The white one, in which white
kids were bludgeoned and scolded about their

"whiteness," and the "kids of color" group, where nonwhite kids were encouraged to blame whiteness for everything that ails them.

At Arizona State University, a course originally called "U.S. Race Theory & the Problem of Whiteness" is returning under the slightly more benign-sounding name "Whiteness and U.S. Race Theory," but rest assured that the gist of the course will remain that "whiteness" is "problematic."

A black history professor in Oregon loudly proclaims that the world would be better without "whiteness," and he still has a job.

For two decades running, a cabal of overwhelmingly white teachers congregates annually to bask in self-loathing and self-flagellation during a "White Privilege Conference," which unspooled hilariously in 2016 when nonwhite attendees started kvetching that the whole affair was too white.

A black female poet named Claudia Rankine announced in October 2016 that she intends to spend $625,000 of her MacArthur Genius Grant to study "whiteness" and teach the white and black sheep that "it's important that people begin to understand that whiteness is not inevitable, and that white dominance is not inevitable."

In the overwhelmingly white yet overwhelmingly anti-white—that happens a lot in academic and editorial circles these days—Huffington Post, a white woman writes "I Sometimes Don't Want to Be White Either" as she pens one long self-congratulatory screed about how good she feels about the fact that she doesn't feel good about herself.

Writing for a Seattle radio station, a trio of extraordinarily white people tells other whites that "it's time to realize you're white," adding that to think you are "just a human being like everyone else" is "deeply rooted in racism."

Not to be outdone in the realm of ethnomasochistic virtue-signaling, a white Afrikaner writes that "Whiteness is like herpes":

> I have whiteness. I didn't know what it was and didn't know what damage it did. But I do know now. I understand and acknowledge all the harm that I and others like me did, even without realising it. I am sorry for the way that things were and are. I accept whiteness exists in me, and am willing to talk about it, and listen as to how it affects others, so that those effects may be reduced and one day eradicated.

Um, I have whiteness, too. But I realize that unlike herpes, we wouldn't even have a modern world without whiteness.

The creeps who started the whole notion of "whiteness" as a pathology are the usual motley crew of self-hating whites and white-hating nonwhites. Some trace it back to black writers such as W. E. B. Du Bois ("The discovery of a personal whiteness among the world's peoples is a very modern thing") and James Baldwin ("As long as you think you are white, there's no hope for you.")

But "Whiteness Studies" metastasized as a pseudo-academic vocation with the help of the aggressively self-loathing Theodore W. Allen (author of *The Invention of the White Race*) and genocidal anti-white insect Noel Ignatiev, who helms a group known as Race Traitor whose goal is to "abolish the white race."

And such loathsome, idiotic, masochistic mental cases are what pass for academics these days.

Since whiteness is only accepted as a synonym for "evil," the academic discipline known as "whiteness studies" is a nonstop onslaught against all things white. As neocon grumpy-puss David Horowitz once told a reporter:

> *Black studies celebrates blackness, Chicano studies celebrates Chicanos, women's studies celebrates women and white studies attacks white people as evil.*

As I've said many times but will keep saying until it seeps into everyone's impossibly thick skulls, the most powerful political weapon is guilt. It can disable entire populations without a single shot being fired. Apparently those who are constantly injecting the collective white unconscious with guilt serum are deathly afraid of what white people could accomplish if they were to toss their "invisible knapsacks" of imaginary guilt into the nearest river.

Modern white people are in thrall to a massive collective guilt complex the likes of which the world may have never known. I'd be fascinated to see historical precedents of entire populations being brainwashed into self-hatred merely for being more successful and technologically advanced than other groups. Whichever team wins the World Series this year, I doubt they'll chalk it up to "unearned privilege."

Psst—white people: There is no shame in being white. There is only shame in ever thinking there was.

2

The Problem With White Guys These Days

Hey, what the heck is wrong with white guys these days?

It's easy to find people eager to answer that question. I'll spotlight four recent essays—two from white authors, two from blacks.

The gender split among these four scribes is three guys and only one girl because, when you get right down to brass tacks, I don't feel that women deserve equal rights.

Jerrod Laber is 100% hu-white right down to the bone, from his blue eyes to his thin lips to his straight blond hair. But I suspect that if Jerrod were able, he'd crawl right out of his white skin and replace it with any pigmentation that was urine-colored or darker.

"White males in Generation Z aren't that woke after all," Laber bemoans in a *Washington Examiner* piece about how young white males are kinda, like, racist and sexist assholes just like their daddies and their daddies' daddies were.

(In case you were unaware, "woke" is a term used by urban teens to describe a mental state in which one believes they are cognizant of how the world really works but instead wouldn't have a clue if it slapped them in the face. Saying that someone is "woke" is a hip way of saying that they suffer from late-stage Dunning-Kruger effect.)

Laber says that white men—himself excluded, I'm assuming—are prone to racism and denial and delusions of persecution. He says nothing more of substance than that they're bad people who should feel bad about this fact, which eventually will be the only way they'll possibly feel good about themselves, although he can't guarantee anything.

He says he wants to have an "honest discourse about race," but I suspect that it'd take only about a minute of real honesty about race to have him melting like a candle.

Another white guy who has a problem with white guys these days is music critic Daniel Johanson. I've stared at his picture for an hour and still have no idea *what* this guy is. He says he's white—actually, it's more like he *confesses* that he's white—but he must be using a very broad definition of the term. If I had to venture a guess, I'd reckon he's part-Lebanese, part-Ewok. Still, he says he's white, so I'll do the decent thing and hold him accountable for every last sin of his forefathers.

Daniel recently penned a bold and trailblazing essay called "Classical Music's White Male Supremacy is Overt, Pervasive, and a Problem" in some magazine I've never heard of before and hope to never hear of again. In Dan's extended lamentation, he takes music made by white males in a white-male environment to task for being, you know, too white-maley.

Lest you get any weird ideas, Mr. Johanson wants to inform you that he is a white man but is NOT happy about it one bit:

> *As a white man, there have been and continue to be countless times in which I have needed to recognize that privilege, white supremacy, homophobia, toxic masculinity, and gender normativity are layered issues. It's easy to call a Nazi a racist because they are so obviously a racist. Not all racists are willing to take up that mantle.*

I gotta tell you: The way he describes it, it sounds positively exhausting to be a white man.

As a white man, Daniel Johanson has a bone to pick with all those dead white men who composed all those dead white symphonies, as if poor black Americans are threatening to burn down cities from coast to coast if they aren't allowed easier access to opera music.

Have you ever met a black person that didn't love opera music? I haven't. And when I say that, I mean that I've never asked any black people about it. It's one of those topics that you instinctually know not to raise with them because they'd probably laugh in your face.

"Recognizing that Classical Music has implied White Supremacy for centuries is hard for those that study the art form," Johanson ululates. Actually, it's easy to recognize for anyone who realizes that it's almost exclusively a white male art form. You may get the occasional 65-pound chick from Asia who can play the hell out of a fiddle, but she's merely an exception and a token and classical music is fundamentally a white-guy thing, which is why you wouldn't understand.

Johanson's piece referenced a recent *Washington Post* essay in which some white broad lamented that classical music was "white bread"—she actually used that phrase three times—and looked forward to a day when the classical-music scene became more "colorful" and wasn't just "just devoted to works by the same white men."

Again—these people seem to think that if your average urban black male is denied early exposure to the works of Vivaldi, he may lose all hope and turn to a life of crack cocaine and endless gunplay.

White men can't seem to stop causing problems for others. Not only are they destroying classical music, they're ruining the moods of black people across the country. Day after day, black bloggers openly scorn white men for harshing their mellow.

Over at The Good Men Project—which is a website that teaches the only good men are those who've been completely stripped of their manhood—a black man with the wonderfully Founding Father-y name of Franklin Madison scolds white males *en masse* for tryin' to pull some bullshit and claim they ain't racist. "You, White Males, Don't Get to Define Whether You Are Racist or Not," Madison lectures us white males in a manner that we would be racist for suggesting might not only be condescending, but also a little controlling.

"What's it going to take for white men to start talking about race?" Madison asks.

Is he serious? I can't *stop* talking about it. I could talk about it for 24 hours straight enabled only by Gatorade and a will to prevail. But unlike Mr. Madison, I believe I understand the difference between a discussion and a lecture:

> *Because you are embedded in the power structure by birth and the color of your skin, only the oppressed get to make that determination. It doesn't help your case if you say, "I am not a racist" just that statement alone lends credence to the fact that you probably are, you just have been too insensitive to know otherwise.*

Sounds like a lecture to me, Satchmo. Can we all get along? No, not when you're acting like a dick.

Donyae Coles—who appears to be quite fat—insists that even the "'GOOD' WHITE PEOPLE SILENCE PEOPLE OF COLOR EVERY DAY"—that's right, even the *good* ones. Day after day across this nation that reeks to high heaven with extraordinarily stinky racism, even the good white people are walking straight up to random black people and telling them they better shut their fat black mouths if they know what's good for them.

Donyae—no comment on the name there—says that her genocide is bigger than white genocide, and therefore white people need to acknowledge their deep guilt and shame in their completely unconscious role in propping up systemic networks of racism and oppression and I'm really making all of this up because I only took a glance at her article and could tell where all of it was going.

I pass no judgment on Franklin Madison or Donyae Coles for two simple reasons:

1. They're black;

2. They aren't white.

I *expect* them to say negative things about white people. It's like, you know, they're members of another football team. A modicum of shit-talking is expected.

As for the two white guys, I rain down thunderous and unforgiving judgment upon their soft heads. For all they want to prattle on about what's wrong with white guys these days, all they need to do is look in the mirror.

The problem with white guys these days is that they think there's something wrong with being white guys. Once they solve that problem, the rest will be a breeze.

3

Let's All Tell More "White People" Jokes!

What's the deal with white people? [the almost entirely white audience laughs]

I mean, right—like, what the hell? [more laughter]

Like, I mean, we've told nothing BUT "white people" jokes for the past two generations while we've socially lynched anyone who tells jokes about all other groups, but why are white people still so thin-skinned that they can't take a joke? [laughter, cont.]

Who doesn't realize that white people can't dance and that they love mayonnaise and that they smell like wet dogs? [laughter]

And isn't it a form of hilariously beautiful justice that they're not having babies and are going to be wiped out over the next hundred years? [everyone laughs except one audience member, who shouts, "Hey, that sounds racist!"]

Ladies and gentlemen, we've found our Klansman in the audience! [audience roars with laughter, then begins physically attacking the "Klansman"]

Writer Chris Mohney is one of the goodwhites. Or so he would have you believe. It appears that by his own admission, Chris is Jewish, and therefore a recent article he wrote for NBC News in which he stoops to address other whites in his role as "a fellow white person" falls in line with a long tradition of Jewish people writing condescending open letters lecturing their "fellow white people" about their innate awfulness. Such essays have proliferated to the point where they've become a meme of their own. So if Chris is actually white, it's with a strict qualification that tends to ameliorate much of the heavy, heavy guilt burden—he's carrying a Jew Card in his wallet at all times.

I'm sure he's fine with anti-Jewish jokes. Just kidding—*that* was a joke!

Mohney's article was titled "Are 'white people' jokes racist? Let a fellow white person explain." He acts as if he cares about his "fellow white people" and gently explains that anti-white jokes "can be a jarring experience if you're not used to being made fun of."

Not used to being made fun of? White people would probably have to go back to sometime in the mid-1960s to recall a time when they *weren't* constantly being mocked. Young white people, especially, were born into a world where whites were the ONLY people it was OK to mock. Not only can one's career be ruined by mocking nonwhites, one risks eternal social pariah status merely for pointing out the double standard. For those in media, mocking white people is a form of career advancement, as we all learned when *The New York Times* hired Sarah Jeong despite—or maybe because of—her history of staying virulently anti-white things.

But Chris Mohney, possibly aware that an outlet such as NBC News wouldn't touch him if he dared note that the double standard is real and potentially dangerous, appears to be yet another zombie who's gullibly swallowed the Zen koan that states "It's impossible to be racist against white people." He also seems to think it's impossible for white people to have ever been slaves, as for some unknown reason he found a need to cite *The New York Times'* effort to "debunk" the "myth" of Irish slaves, an effort which was subsequently stomped to death by me and Michael A. Hoffman II in this book's chapter "White Slavery Denial."

Mohney addresses the Sarah Jeong debacle as a way of further deriding thin-skinned, diaper-wearing whites who can't take a light-hearted joke about their superficial characteristics that wasn't mean-spirited at all and in fact was only a sly way of mocking how mean and abusive white people have been to others throughout history. He said that Jeong's old tweets "make fun of white people in various ways," yet he focuses on the ones about how white people sunburn easily and might have to live underground like goblins. The closest he comes to addressing Jeong's more malignant tweets was when he cited the one about how she took joy in being cruel to old white men, but he deflects that by alleging that the only people who are legitimately cruel to old white men are "other old white men in government."

He insists Jeong's tweets were nothing more a benign attempt to "superficially mock this or that alleged racial characteristic" like, say, a joke about big black lips or slanted Asian eyes might do, even though we all know it's forbidden to mock gigantic black ape lips or tiny, thumb-drive Asian eyes that make them such bad drivers.

The tweets that Mohney sidesteps entirely are the ones where Jeong repeatedly says white people have "no culture," that they invented nothing, that it was her "plan all along" for them to go extinct, and that she posted the hashtag #CancelWhitePeople.

How convenient, fellow "white person"!

He then dives into the extra-convenient role of mind-reader/gaslighter, claiming that he possesses the psychic powers to discern what white people REALLY mean when they dare to notice double standards:

> *White people, even though we don't like to admit it, know that racism isn't just about who you like or don't like. Racism has always been and always will be about possessing, maintaining and applying power.*

No, you dimwit, unlike you, we haven't all swallowed that line of obviously fraudulent sophistry. If the word "racism" is to have any meaning at all, and if we even want to pretend we're going to avoid a cultural civil war, we should keep the word confined to meaning what I was taught it meant when I was a kid—negative feelings or thoughts toward other races. From memory, there was no double standard for about, oh, eighteen months sometime in the mid-1970s, and since then, you can't say a good word about white people or a bad word about anyone else without being socially and financially destroyed.

He further insists that it is ontologically impossible for certain white people to object to such jokes merely on the basis that there is a double standard that excuses them while forbidding all other manner of racist jokes:

> Thus, white people getting mad — or publicly performing anger, at least — about white people jokes is actually white people getting mad about threats to white power....White people all implicitly know that racism is kind of like a pyramid, from which the effects of racism (and the jokes) always roll downhill.

You see that everywhere these days—self-appointed swamis claiming the insight to tell you what people *really* mean despite what they say. It's a way of calling the person a liar while abdicating one's responsibility to factually counteract what they actually said. If you see any writer claiming that someone's statement is "really about" this or that, or that they "really mean this" when they actually said that, confront them about it. This sort of editorial reading of tea leaves has persisted for far too long.

But for the sake of argument, let's say that some white people out there are anxious about losing power. OK, then—name one person in their right mind who feels *good* about losing power or wealth. Name anyone who isn't a self-flagellating masochist who thinks it's a good thing to experience a sharp diminution in wealth, power, resources, and numbers.

Would he have criticized the Comanche for fighting about a perceived loss of power? Would he have dumped on sub-Saharan Africans for objecting to European colonialism? Would he have told Jews in the Middle Ages to quit kvetching about all the pogroms? Not bloody likely—in this framework where whiteness is, was, and forever will be the only bad form of ethnic identity, it's only whites who are commanded to celebrate a loss of power.

What a putz.

He also implies that Sarah Jeong's tweets come from a lower position on this "pyramid" that has whites at the top. Again, that must be why Asians live longer and make far more money than white people in this white-supremacist society, yes? Hello?

He's not listening. Chris says it is "literally impossible, by definition, to be racist against white people, or to tell a racist joke about a white person."

That's because you changed the definition a few years back while we were all asleep. If you had tried peddling that insane double standard back in the

1960s, the Civil Rights movement would have been squashed in under a minute.

4

The Great White War

There is no one I hate more than someone who tries to tell me whom I hate.

For a quarter-century now I've made it very clear that most of my hatred—and there's quite a lot of it, I never run out—is *intra*-racial. While those who have a death grip on media and education would love to pretend that I sit around all day stewing about blacks, I find myself incapable of mustering nearly the sort of searing animus toward my Negroidal brethren that I consistently feel toward liberal white coastal elites, who have their heads planted so far up their own asses and are so drunk on the notion of their moral irreproachability that they can't possibly conceive that anyone would hate them, much less some lowly, foulmouthed plumber's son who grew up in a brick row home and views white liberal pieties as shallow, self-serving extravagances that help no one but themselves—specifically, their self-image.

These are the people who tell me I vote against my interests while they actively spit on my interests.

These are the ones who endorse trade and immigration policies that don't adversely affect them yet have rendered much of working white America hopeless, suicidal, and strung out on pills.

They are the ones who are statistically far more likely to be descended from the white slave-owning class than they are from the far more numerous descendants of white indentured servants, yet they've successfully scapegoated poor whites and left them bearing the brunt of black resentment.

These are the ones who'd like to imagine that Klansmen and skinheads and cops are roaming the streets indiscriminately beating and murdering nonwhites. They are either ignorant of the modern statistics regarding interracial violence or they'll find some half-assed sociological excuse to justify them. Living largely as they do in gated and secure communities, they rarely get their hands dirty with such trifles, anyway.

These are the ones who are cheering the idea that white demographic decline is inevitable, naively believing that the dusky hordes whom they're welcoming in by the millions and among whom they're fanning anti-white resentment will somehow not see *them* as white, too, and thus as just as guilty and deserving of retribution as any meth-smoking, rusty-trailer-dwelling, Alabama hilljack.

In a 2013 article for Taki's Mag, Steve Sailer listed America's four racial groups:

- *Blacks*
- *Bad Whites*
- *Good Whites*
- *Misc.*

John Derbyshire has subsequently fused "good-whites" and "badwhites" into all-purpose terms describing the primary combatants in America's "Cold Civil War":

> ...that is, the everlasting struggle between, on the one hand, the Progressive goodwhites who dominate our country's mainstream culture—the Main Stream Media, the universities and law schools, big corporations, the federal bureaucracy—and, on the other hand, the ignorant gap-toothed hillbilly redneck badwhites clinging to their guns and religion out on the despised margins of civilized society.

Another blogger sketches out a rough delineation between goodwhites and badwhites:

Goodwhite: a White involved in an inter-racial marriage, with mixed-race children, who vigorously defends and promotes race-mixing, who is very pro-Jewish, and who is suitably hostile to White nationalism. If on "the right"—a good cuckservative.

Badwhite: a White who disapproves of race-mixing, is skeptical of Jewish behavior, and supports White nationalism.

According to former porn industry blogger Luke Ford, only the badwhites don't realize they're in a war:

Only the "bad whites" for the most part do not realize they are in a war. The good whites (Liberals, Leftists, Feminists, Democrats, SJW, SWPL hipsters, Atheists, LGBT, pro-choice advocates, gun control advocates, etc.) are seeking to destroy any and all political power and influence still held by the "bad whites" (Conservatives, Republicans, Libertarians, Christians, red-necks, white nationalists, gun rights advocates, pro-life advocates, heterosexual white males, et al), so the "good whites" will be able to completely have their way in transforming America into a country they believe will be more "just and equal". With them firmly in charge of it all, of course.

It has long been my contention that the over-wrought and frankly embarrassing paroxysms of agony and outrage that have followed Donald

Trump's election is nothing more than the good-whites' paranoia that the yahoos have awakened and may be out for blood. Trump may have been born to wealth, but unlike Hillary Clinton (who slammed "deplorables") and Barack Obama (who spoke of bitter clingers and speaks more like a goodwhite than even most goodwhites do), Trump speaks in a vernacular that is badwhite to the core.

Despite the fact that hardly anyone these days is willing to contest the fact that Stalin and Mao killed far more people than Hitler did, they'll still purse their lips, clench their sphincters, and say that Hitler was worse because he didn't kill people for what they thought, but for *who they were*, and his victims had no control over that.

What they overlook is the fact that at least Hitler targeted people who lacked consanguinity with him; Stalin and Mao killed *their own people*, which, in an evolutionary sense, seems like a far deeper betrayal.

And this is what the goodwhites are cheering—the suppression, silencing, displacement, demonization, and in some cases, the outright extermination of people that they are *much more closely related to genetically* than the exotic oppressed racial pets that live tucked far away from them and that they fetishize safely from afar.

Killing a stranger whom you may feel is legitimately threatening you is one thing; fratricide is quite another. And yet the goodwhites seem to feel that their open and gleeful fratricidal malice toward their less fortunate brethren is somehow virtuous rather than hateful.

In her book *Good White People,* Shannon Sullivan takes the sanctimonious middle-class goodwhites to task for projecting their own guilt complexes onto the easily despised and perennially maligned rednecks and white trash.

So far, so good. I appreciate her gesture in calling goodwhite sanctimony out for the self-serving vanity project that it is.

However, she and I reach a fork in the road when she encourages both the goodwhites and badwhites to accept their role in dismantling the "illness" of whiteness and forge ahead hand-in-hand to build a racially just and equitable society—but, as is ALWAYS the case, she offers no timelines or quantifiers for exactly how or why our society is currently unjust, nor any spreadsheets with graphs that will show exactly when "justice" has been achieved and everyone can finally quit whining once and for all. Unlike her, I think it's OK being white. And what the goodwhites don't realize is that I wouldn't care either way if they hadn't beaten me over the head since childhood with the idea that there's *nothing* OK with being white.

If there is to be war in America's streets, there is no group I would more eagerly battle than the goodwhites. They are the tattletales and snitches and teacher's pets of the white race. And unlike many other potential foes—who would probably at least put up a good fight—the goodwhites are far too soft and clueless to face the wrath of the awakened badwhite.

5

The White Guilt Educational Complex

In celebration of Black History Month, the entire student population of a Virginia high school was assembled together in early February 2016 and forced to endure the collective guilt-whipping of a four-minute cartoon called "Structural Discrimination: The Unequal Opportunity Race."

Produced by the African American Policy Forum—which is not a racist organization, because, duh, African Americans cannot possibly be racist—the crudely animated propaganda piece depicts four runners pitted against one another in a track race. A white male, a white female, a brownish male, and a full-blown coal-black dreadlocked female poise crouched at the starting line.

But when the starting gun goes off, the Sprinters of Color are kept at the starting line by a red light while terms such as SLAVERY, BROKEN TREATIES, GENOCIDE, MANIFEST DESTINY, TRAIL OF TEARS, DRED SCOTT, SEGREGA- TION, CHINESE EXCLUSION ACT, and JAPANESE INTERNMENT fly by their heads.

The nonwhite runners get lapped at least twice before they are allowed to start, but the moment they begin running, dark storm clouds form over their heads to impede their progress. Again they face injustices such as DISCRIMINATION, POOR SCHOOLING, and UNDEREMPLOY- MENT.

Unlike the white runners, they are forced to make their way through a shark-infested moat titled STANDARDIZED TESTS. Even though the brownish male survives the life-threatening ordeal of standardized testing, he is suddenly ensnared by the SCHOOL TO PRISON PIPELINE, which cap- tures him in a cage and whisks him away—even though he didn't commit any crime, which is, like, totally unfair!

The dreadlocked black girl soldiers nobly onward until she finally hits a brick wall marked DEAD END as the result of SHORTENED LIFESPAN. This is a curious alibi for the black woman's failure considering that in America, black women outlive white men.

The only two runners who complete the race are, but of course, the white male and female, the latter of whom comes in second because the male speeds by her on a conveyor belt due to CONNECTIONS and PRIVILEGE and WEALTH and the OLD BOY NETWORK.

The final message that splashes on the screen is AFFIRMATIVE ACTION HELPS LEVEL THE PLAYING FIELD.

The film does not bother to attempt explaining why, despite the Chinese Exclusion Act and Japanese internment, Asian Americans outperform white Americans both on standardized tests and in terms of per-capita income, but let's not get carried away and allow facts to undermine what is otherwise a carefully crafted propaganda piece designed to provide alibis for seemingly intractable black underperformance in these areas.

The screening of this white-bashing video is hardly an aberration. At times it seems as if the White Guilt Industrial Complex is more firmly entrenched in American academia than are trivialities such as reading, writing, and arithmetic.

You will now kindly purge from your mind the idea that this may in some way be related to the fact that American test scores are falling. You must also restrain yourself from pausing to consider that the general thrust of American education these days is not to fill minds with new ideas, but to cleanse them of all *unacceptable* ideas, no matter how logical, natural, and instinctual those ideas may be.

From preschool all the way through to grad school, American academia is no longer a world of education, but of indoctrination.

It's where seventh-graders are required to read "White Privilege: Unpacking the Invisible Knapsack."

Where a Common Core-endorsed book called *The Jacket* explains to fourth-graders how a racist white boy named Phil wrongly assumes that it was a black kid who stole his brother's jacket, even though, if you want to get all racist and technical, black Americans are statistically overrepresented in property crime.

It is a magical world where crude, pseudoreligious parables of collective guilt and intergenerational racial karma substitute for math and verbal skills.

It's where everything is the fault of whites and nothing is the fault of nonwhites. Low black test scores and high black dropout rates? Blame white racism. High suspension rates for black grade schoolers and high schoolers? It can't possibly be linked to disproportionate black misbehavior—blame it on white racism again.

The modern American classroom is where the only acceptable explanation for stubborn educational and financial disparities between whites and non-whites is white racism, because genetics obviously couldn't possibly have anything to do with it.

It's where teachers routinely flock to conferences dedicated to "Interrupting Whiteness" and smashing "White Privilege." Where nonwhite students are encouraged to segregate themselves in racial special-interest groups that focus on pride, whereas whites are only encouraged to gather together in order to "dismantle white supremacy." Where the world's unofficial encyclopedia embraces all forms of racial pride except one—Wikipedia's definition of "White pride" is the only one that uses the word "racist," whereas it gives all other forms of racial pride a pass.

It's where white moms publicly pat themselves on the back for penning ethnomasochistic screeds such as "Raising White Children to be Anti-Racist Allies" and "It's My Job to Raise Children Who

Are Not Only Not Racist But Actively Anti-Racist."

It's where government agencies throw millions of working class whites' taxpayer dollars at cocka-mamie race pimps such as Glenn Singleton, a black man whose Pacific Educational Group peddles Critical Race Theory gibberish in 184 American school districts.

Where Jane Elliott, described as "the Torquemada of thought reform," rakes in untold cash and is lauded by Oprah Winfrey and Ellen Degeneres because she forces white students to cry as she cru-elly guides them through public humiliation rituals that are a hybrid of communist Chinese struggle sessions and the Stanford Prison Experiment.

It's a logically impossible world where somehow society is rooted in white supremacy, yet this same society's cardinal sin is white supremacy.

It's a world of ceaseless propagandistic demoraliza-tion that cumulatively constitutes systematic ideo-logical child abuse against white children.

It's definitely a different world than the one I inhab-ited when I went to school. In my Catholic grade school, a female "lay" teacher—they're called that because they're allowed to get laid—once specu-lated that blacks look more like apes than whites do because they are less evolved than whites. In high school, a nun—they're called that because they don't *get* none—told us that black poverty was due to the fact that blacks are impulsive and don't comprehend the principle of delayed gratification.

When my son was only three and in preschool, his first-ever homework assignment had nothing to do with the alphabet or numerals. Instead, he was assigned to do a presentation on a black historical figure of his choice.

I'll spend the rest of my life helping him get the best education possible. But first I have to help him unlearn everything they teach him in school.

6

The Difference Between White People and Black People

Imagine for a moment that you are an intelligent and self-sufficient Martian living in a plush, temperature-controlled trailer home somewhere amid the vast frozen plains of that lonely red planet. Also imagine that through the miracle of advanced Martian technology, you have Internet access—it could even be AOL, it doesn't really matter. Let's also pretend that your curious, veiny, overdeveloped Martian brain, despite its better instincts, has become fascinated with those foolish simian earthling humanoids, particularly the "white people" and "black people" who inhabit what will be known for a little while longer as the United States of America.

Since you are a Martian, you have no childishly naïve prejudices—nor any meticulously acquired adult postjudices—about frivolities such as "racism" or "injustice" or "equality." You merely want to know the difference between white people and black people, and to keep it "relevant" as the teen earthlings are fond of saying, you confine your search to the prior week's news. You search the phrases "white people" and "black people" over the preceding seven Earth days.

What would you learn?

You would learn that white people are a uniquely self-loathing breed who not only openly question whether they can be trusted—they come right out and *say* they can't be trusted.

They blame themselves rather than blacks for the ceaseless black-white evolutionary conflict that white earthlings self-deprecatingly refer to as "racism." They chide other white people for not allowing black people to constantly lecture them. They encourage double standards that claim it's "racist" and harmful when white people wear blackface but entirely benign when black people dress in whiteface.

Turning the former slave master's whip upon their own kind, they constantly flog themselves over a past when they acted in collective self-interest rather than collective self-denial, and somehow they see this as virtuous and bold rather than masochistic and pathetic. They manage to view it as a sign of progress rather than decline. They're a strange alien breed, indeed.

They revel in lampooning their own supposed cultural awkwardness, in using the word "whitest" as a pejorative, and in constantly claiming that whites are continually "stealing" and "appropriating" things from blacks—inane and ultimately insubstantial things such as a fondness for large posteriors, since apparently there isn't much in the way of true scientific innovations to appropriate.

They love when black people make fun of them and perpetually chide them for racism and call them "crazy" and "jokingly" rub racial double standards right in their faces. They even think it's cute and adorable when self-loathing white radicals gather black kids from a dysfunctional war zone together to film a video mocking white people for their cluelessness. They especially enjoy it when black people, no matter how openly resentful and hate-filled they are toward whites, piously claim that it's impossible for blacks to be racist.

OK, then, what would a curious Martian's quick Internet search of the past week tell them about black people?

The eager, fact-seeking Martian would learn that white people have historically hated black people and have conditioned the poor black bastards to hate themselves. Life has been unfair and oppressive for black people ever since being kidnapped from their homeland, despite the fact that by most measures of living standards such as longevity and yearly income and access to medical care, it is far better in America for them than it is back in their homeland.

Black people face racism and hatred everywhere they turn, whether it comes to dating, interacting with police, being terrorized by the state, being subjected to a war of occupation by the demon sons of Yacub, or allowing record companies to wage an ongoing campaign of genocide against them. Even millionaire female athletes still have to slog through the occasional racist remark.

Since black people are viewed as inferior, they live in horrible communities and face ceaseless oppression and hatred at the hands of bigoted politicians who use them as tools but don't really care about them, who only serve to buttress and enrich racist policemen and a racist prison system that routinely sets them up on false charges, making them insane while refusing to treat them for mental illness.

Surveying all the available evidence—at least as it's framed through a Google search of the past week's American media—a discerning Martian would reach two sobering and inescapable conclusions:

1) Being white sucks because white people suck.
2) Being black sucks because white people suck.

One might also rightly develop the sense that white people should hate themselves and be forced to live a bleak existence of constant apology and retreat. One might also conclude that black people have every right to bleed resentment from every pore until this dangerously unquantifiable, highly emotional, and uniquely human notion of "justice" is achieved.

Since you are a highly rational Martian, you would also be led to the inexorable conclusion that the current situation, whether by accident or design, cannot possibly lead to racial harmony. Instead, it almost seems purposely engineered to result in escalating levels of conflict.

Any sane Martian would conclude it's better to stay on the red planet and let those silly black-and-white earthlings sort this one out for themselves.

7

"We're White, We're Male, and We Suck!"

American culture reached Peak Beta during one sad week in May 2012 when three privileged white-male pundits wrote essays declaring that privileged white males suck.

Lifelong morbidly obese bitchy lesbian Roger Ebert apparently dismantled the presumably elaborate series of pulleys and harnesses that enable him to orally service his adiposely domineering, melanin-drenched wife in order to run that half-a-mouth of his about how "Women Are Better Than Men." Amazingly, Ebert became privy to this startling epiphany while watching a movie about how women are better than men. Ebert, who was apparently born without male hormones, decried "testosterone." He intimated that men, at least the brawny ones, are as obsolete as farm animals and that women will be better suited to take command of "our emerging world economy":

> *Women are nicer than men. And the sooner more of them take positions of power, the better our chances as a species.*

Mr. Ebert has obviously never heard of Aileen Wuornos or Elizabeth Báthory.

Ebert's verbal genuflection before the Giant Invisible Goddess Vulva is nothing new. Nor was it as cringeworthy as other recent spectacles of public male self-neutering such as the unconsciously hysterical, vagina-dessiccating "Dear Woman" video compiled by a group of ex-men offering "a collective apology on behalf of their gender." It wasn't as abjectly self-deballing as the recent trend of progressive boy hamsters holding "I Am a Feminist Because..." placards in what appear to be last-ditch attempts to get laid. It is merely the latest example in a decades-long tradition of men taking pride in taking shame in being men.

The second male scribe to fire a flaming Roman candle into his own crotch that week in May 2012 was the profoundly unhandsome sci-fi writer John Scalzi, who apparently attracts legions of profoundly unhandsome fans who could pass for the bastard sons of Roger Ebert, all of them swinging their flaccid lightsabers of righteous self-abnegation in agreement. Scalzi, who claims he's in the process of writing a video game, used his undoubtedly well-manicured fingers to peck out an essay called "Straight White Male: The Lowest Difficulty Setting There Is." Since he apparently spends much of his life lost amid fantasies, he likened American social hierarchies to a video game where being born a white male makes the game easier than it is for anyone else.

Rounding out that week's triumvirate of white-male auto-castrati was HuffPo contributor Bob Cesca, who not only acknowledged a media double standard when it comes to reporting interracial violence—he defended it! He insisted that the double standard "*has to* remain"—his italics—to help dismantle "the white-dominated American power structure" until that day in the distant future when we finally reach "full equality." Despite the mountains of narrative-subverting evidence that have leaked out in the Trayvon Martin case ever since the media tried peddling him as a Skittle-nibbling cherub, Cesca still says that he and other sensitive white males "can understand why African American activists like Al Sharpton and others are outraged." Apparently he can also understand how Sharpton still retains a pinkie-fingernail's worth of credibility after Tawana Brawley, the Duke Lacrosse scandal, the Crown Heights riots, the Jena

6, and now the Trayvon case, because I don't understand it at all.

Many modern white males appear to have been culturally conditioned to fit themselves with electric dog collars that deliver sharp, painful jolts when they so much as think of offending anyone who isn't a white male. And somehow they seem to see this as noble and brave rather than fearful and compliant. But these self-flagellating public displays are reminiscent of the magical thinking in what I diagnose in another chapter as "Passover Syndrome"—it's as if by declaring that they share in an unpaid collective debt, maybe they can emerge unscathed without having to sacrifice anything tangible beyond their basic dignity.

"I am a privileged white male; that is simply a fact."

"I Am a Privileged White Male...And honestly, sometimes I wish I wasn't."

"...I am a privileged white male; it is easy for me to rationalize my views on races simply because I have it so good."

"I am a formerly clueless privileged white male, who has taken advantage of my privilege....I'm pathetic."

"I am a privileged white male Westerner who is not, and never will be, personally affected by this use of colonizing language...."

"I am a privileged white male...and so I ask the viewer to laugh at me laughing at myself."

Oh, I'm laughing. Laughing and laughing and laughing and laughing. You say that collective pride is a sign of ignorance but that collective shame is a sign of enlightenment. You affirm yourself through self-negation. You think it's brave to be a pussy. You've raised your consciousness so high, you've left planet Earth entirely. You're *hilarious!*

Just as I can't see all this invisible racism, and just as I think that anyone who believes in institutional racism ought to be institutionalized, I'm absolutely blind to all this privilege I allegedly enjoy due to my skin and gender. I don't see the privilege in being required to passively accept my nonexistent role in historical atrocities. I don't see the upside of being constantly lampooned and demonized in media and education. And I definitely don't see the privilege in being a white-male writer in a modern media milieu where it's a career-killer if the first words out of your mouth aren't, "I'm a white male, and I'm sorry."

8

The White Man's Unbearable Burden

Author Niklesh Shukla—a fat brown man who appears to sweat a lot—was named one of *Foreign Policy* magazine's "100 Global Thinkers of 2016." He won this award for his work focusing on the "unbearable whiteness of publishing." Ironically, his surname is a word of Sanskrit origin meaning "white."

In books such as *The Good Immigrant*, the British citizen complains that British society is unfairly dominated by indigenous Britons.

I think I'll move to India, bitch about how the Indian publishing industry is stacked in favor of Indians, and then expect to receive grants and awards...or maybe not.

I've never read a word this chubby *samosa* has written and I never intend to, but the mere fact that he cribbed the already severely overused term "unbearable whiteness" suggests to me that he is an unoriginal hack. This play on Milan Kundera's *Unbearable Lightness of Being* is approaching *Fear and Loathing in...* levels of overuse.

Referring to "whiteness" as "unbearable" is not a bold move if you want a media career these days. In fact, it appears to be a prerequisite.

The Huffington Post—which is owned by a woman who's so white, her eyes appear to be turning into cocaine—is a serial abuser of this term. Her publication decries "The Unbearable Whiteness of Trumpistan," "The Unbearable Whiteness Of Being in China," "The Unbearable Whiteness of Anti-Intellectualism," and "The Unbearable Whiteness of Suicide-by-Mass-Murder." Someone needs to tell the author of the last piece—a beta dweeb named Michael Kimmel who has been described as "the world's most prominent male feminist"—that despite the myth that mass shooters are disproportionately white, a study of mass shooters from 1982 to 2016 reveals that when it comes to this crime, as is the case with nearly all other categories of criminal malfeasance, whites are statistically underrepresented, comprising a mere 57% of the total. Blacks actually perform slightly above their quotient of the population when it comes to mass shootings, but this is to be expected since the subject is crime.

To my knowledge, the quintessentially unbearable writers for the Huffington Post have never referred to blackness or Jewishness as "unbearable."

Despite the fact that the publishing industry slavishly caters to minoritarian tyrants and routinely bashes the very notion of white people, many insist that this industry, too, is unbearably white. A gay black author whinges about "The Unbearable Whiteness of Science Fiction." An editor for the *Islamic Monthly* takes issue with "The Unbearable Whiteness of Canadian Columnists." (He notes that "Canadian columnists are predominately white" and designates this as a "problem.")

A writer for *The American Prospect* slams "The Unbearable Whiteness of Liberal Media," noting that even the staff of *The Nation* has only "slightly over 4 percent of its staff hailing from racial and ethnic minority groups." (Apparently he counts Jews as white.) And of course, even *The Nation* itself bemoans the publishing industry's "unbearable whiteness."

Writing in *TIME*, a certain Eliza Berman tut-tuts "The Unbearable Whiteness of the Oscar Nominations." In the Daily Beast, an Asian woman takes issue with "The Unbearable Whiteness of Cameron Crowe's 'Aloha.'" And Think Progress—which is bankrolled by Holocaust enabler George Soros—has a bone to pick with Ridley Scott's *Moses* and its "Unbearable Whiteness."

These hard-hitting, truth-digging articles all point to a cultural crisis, because it is an undeniable statistical fact that Hollywood's ownership is too white—the proof is in Joel Stein's *LA Times* essay, "Who Runs Hollywood? C'mon."

American music, alas, is likewise condemned as unbearably white. We are lectured about "The Unbearable Whiteness of Soft Rock" and read earnestly stupid attempts to explain "Why 'Indie' Music Is So Unbearably White."

In the real world, nine out of the top ten singles currently on the Billboard charts are by black artists. But I wouldn't hold my breath waiting for a barrage of articles about the music industry's "Unbearable Blackness."

TV, too, is allegedly so white that it makes people want to scream. At Salon, a certain Scott Timberg slammed David Letterman's farewell shows for their "unbearable whiteness." Failed black late-night host Kamau Bell has a problem with "The Unbearable Whiteness of Late Night." And *The Advocate* feels the need to cry little rainbow tears about the "Unbearable Whiteness Behind *Orange Is the New Black*."

Of course, black actors are actually overrepresented on major network shows—and *severely* overrepresented on commercials—but let's not let facts get in the way of an egregiously self-righteous and hyper-emotional narrative, shall we?

Politics? Unbearably white as well! This includes Bernie Sanders, the American left, protesters, Congress, and America's donor class.

Regarding the political donor class, *Jewish Business News* claims that "US Jews Contribute 50% Of All Donations To The Democratic Party And 25% To The Republican Party." How unbearably white of them!

Everywhere you look, you'll see something unbearably white. This includes marijuana legalization, baseball, brunch, milk, librarians, and craft beer.

It all reminds me of a brilliant exchange between Anthony Jeselnik—that rare Nordic-looking funnyman—and black comic Patrice O'Neal at the Comedy Central Roast of Charlie Sheen:

Anthony Jeselnik: Besides, what can you say about Mike Tyson that hasn't already been a title of a Richard Pryor album?
Patrice O'Neal: Oh shit.
Anthony Jeselnik: He got it. Patrice got it.
Patrice O'Neal: Too many white people [in the audience] to get that.
Anthony Jeselnik: Too many white people? You know what no one ever says? Too few black people.

Would that it were true. But the iron template these days is to complain that in *everything*, there are way too many whites and far too few blacks.

You know what's truly unbearable about white people these days? That they don't find this non-stop defamation unbearable. I'd honestly like to see a historical antecedent to what's currently going on in America, where a majority population is broadly slandered every second of every day, but precious few of them are even bold enough to mention it, much less start slandering back.

What puts lie to this notion that "whiteness" is unbearable is the fact that global immigration patterns show nonwhites desperately trying to get into white countries, whereas an inverse phenomenon—say, whites moving to Swaziland in droves—doesn't exist AT ALL in the real world.

If you can't bear all this whiteness, I suggest you run as far away from white people as your soft brown feet will take you. Failing that, I suggest you show some respect toward your mostly unwilling hosts, because it appears that they are rapidly beginning to find *you* unbearable.

9

Dear White People: Stop Apologizing

All across America, white people are apologizing to black people for things they didn't do and for historical situations they had no hand in creating. While it obviously makes these self-flagellating Caucasoids feel good about themselves, will it make even the tiniest difference in the lives of ordinary black Americans?

In Chicago—where blacks and Hispanics comprise 96% of murderers and a similar quotient of murder victims—a phenotypically white and extremely mannish-looking woman named Laurella Willis has been walking all over the Windy City's notoriously murderous South Side toting a poster that says BLACK AMERICA I'M SORRY!! She reportedly traverses those mean streets for 20 miles a day, apologizing her ample ass off to anyone who'll listen. One black resident told a reporter, "It's very touching. Especially someone who's not colored."

Although Willis apparently has no trouble with multiple news sources describing her as "white," on her Facebook page she appears to have fallen under the impression that she's black:

> ..."WE", meaning the black race won't come together to support each other so HOW we gonna have change anywhere else? THAT is trick of the enemy! The devil DOES NOT want u to REALLY unite & STAY united!! Long as Black on black crime continues THE DEVIL has won bcuz your focus has been shifted from the TRUE issue! EQUALITY!!!

So...you want to become equal with the "devil"? I'm not sure I understand the reasoning, if any, here. And what if the true issue isn't equality, but rather innate and intractable inequalities engineered by the grand magnificent process of evolution? What do you do then? How many apologetic sandwich boards will it take to correct nature's inexorable processes?

It appears that Willis's "I'M SORRY!!" poster—as well as Willis, it's hard to tell from behind—made an appearance at the funeral of 310-pound convicted pedophile Alton Sterling, who was shot dead by police after he struggled with them while toting an unlicensed gun on his person. Al Sharpton and Jesse Jackson also appeared at Sterling's funeral, their blowfish-shaped mouths farting out the same sanctimonious and innumerate coffin-riding nonsense that has made them rich beyond most black people's wildest dreams.

Sterling's death—which never would have happened if he hadn't struggled and hadn't been carrying a gun—was mentioned in a viral poem by a certain Pastor Savannah Martin of Tampa, a white woman who was invited onto CNN to pontificate about her weepy videotaped apology for white privilege that she'd set to rhyme:

> I wasn't born rich, but don't get it twisted
> See how I look, my white skin is my privilege.
> I don't get watched when I go to the mall.
> If I get stopped for a ticket, it doesn't end in a brawl....
> I don't know anyone murdered for selling cigs or CDs
> I've never been choked out or shot at by corrupt men in PDs.

Of course, anyone who's remotely sane realizes that Sterling was not "murdered for selling...CDs," nor for being black, but righteous public displays of virtue-signaling have always operated independently of facts.

When he delivered his spoken-word poem, a 14-year-old Jewish boy from Atlanta named Royce Mann became an Internet celebrity after a video of his "White Boy Privilege" performance went viral. Choice bits from that "poem":

> *Dear women, I'm sorry. Dear black people, I'm sorry. Dear Asian-Americans, dear Native Americans, dear immigrants who come here seeking a better life, I'm sorry.*

> *Dear everyone who isn't a middle or upper class white boy, I'm sorry. I have started life on the top of the ladder while you were born on the first rung....*

> *It is embarrassing that we tell our kids that it is not their personality, but instead those same chromosomes that get to dictate what color clothes they wear and how short they must cut their hair. But most of all, it is embarrassing that we deny this. That we claim to live in an equal country, an equal world.*

Keep me out of your "we," kid. I never claimed "we" live in an equal world. I believe the stubborn delusion that we're all equal is the main source of modern social problems.

Writing for Huffington Post, a Jewish woman named Karen Fleshman—who calls herself a "White Woman" and works as a "Diversity and Inclusion Strategist [and] Race Educator"—penned a "Love Letter" to America's "Black Folks:

Dear Black Folks,

When I realized the magnitude of the damage my people have done to yours, I felt guilty for [a] good long time.

My ancestors bought and sold and tormented and discriminated against your ancestors setting us on different trajectories that continue to in large part determine how we live today. On behalf of my ancestors, I apologize to your ancestors for our brutality.

Apparently it never occurred to this cluelessly meddlesome yenta that whites never would have been able to conquer sub-Saharan blacks if the two groups weren't already on vastly different technological and cultural trajectories.

And so it continues, this nauseating specter of white and questionably white ethnomasochists apologizing to blacks in letters to the editor, on their knees, and even at gunpoint. Why? Merely because they were born into the world's wealthiest nation, EXACTLY LIKE all the blacks to whom they're groveling.

If most American blacks didn't tacitly realize that they have it far better here than they would in their absurdly romanticized Mother Continent, they'd be leaving in droves. Instead, the net migratory pattern remains lopsided heavily from Africa to the USA, not the inverse.

I've been asking this question since the early 1990s and will continue asking it until someone gives a satisfying answer or they throw their hands up and admit there is no answer: Can you name a majority-black country on Earth where blacks live longer and have a higher standard of living than they do in America? Don't avoid the question or wonder about my motives for asking it—just ANSWER it. If you can't, you will be forced to concede that blacks die younger and are far more impoverished when left to their own devices than when they live in white-majority countries. I realize this fact alone destroys your dangerously fraudulent "equality" narrative, but the question must be asked, again and again, wherever poisonous propaganda serves to make white people feel guilty for being history's winners.

Why should whites apologize? For inventing nearly everything and still being spat upon by the ingrates who freely "appropriate" these inventions without even a simple "thank you"?

While all this shirt-rending may make a few people feel better about themselves, as far as I can tell, none of it has made black people more intelligent or less prone to committing crime.

In a sane world, being a historical loser would be seen as a matter of shame rather than a bragging right. In a sane world, being a historical winner would never be cause for masochistic public displays of self-abnegation. But that world no longer exists. As the English mystic Noddy Holder once said, the whole world's goin' crazee.

I've seen countless white people apologize for doing better than blacks in America. What I've never *once* seen is Asians, Indians, or Jews apologizing to white Americans for outperforming them financially and on standardized tests. The *only* racial group in America so deeply in the thrall of self-hatred is white America. This suggests that they've been hoodwinked by one of the most massive and comprehensive propaganda-fueled collective mindfucks in history.

Self-hatred is not a virtue; it's a sickness.

White people of the world, stop apologizing. You have nothing to lose if you stop and everything to lose if you don't.

10

Laughing About White Genocide

On Christmas Eve 2016, an eminently smackable-looking self-described "actual communist" crouched down, grabbed his ankles, and shat the following Tweet upon planet Earth:

All I want for Christmas is White Genocide

The offending tweeter was George Ciccariello-Maher, a professor of politics and global studies at Philadelphia's Drexel University. He doubled down on Christmas Day:

To clarify: when the whites were massacred during the Haitian Revolution, that was a good thing indeed.

But in the midst of a backlash, he said he was just kidding because—haw!—there's no such thing as white genocide:

> On Christmas Eve, I sent a satirical tweet about an imaginary concept, 'white genocide'...an idea invented by white supremacists and used to denounce everything from interracial relationships to multicultural policies....It is a figment of the racist imagination.

Ciccariello-Maher's own words—in which he repeatedly takes a sadistic glee in the notion of violent white extinction—reveal he is absolutely full of shit. He wrote a 2014 paper called "So Much the Worse for the Whites': Dialectics of the Haitian Revolution" in which he argues that the wholesale slaughter of Haiti's white inhabitants was a righteous act leading toward "universal emancipation," and we all know how well that all worked out for Haiti.

In 2013, the mystifyingly employed professor stated "Yacub made a lot of white folks," citing the Nation of Islam's brain-damaged theory that an evil black professor created white people roughly 6,000 years ago.

In 2015, he wrote, "Abolish the White Race."

In 2016 he wrote about an alleged conversation with his son, whom daddy has apparently brainwashed to the point where sonny-boy is talking about poisoning white people. Late in the year Ciccariello-Maher wrote about sending "Racist Crackers" to gulags.

Pardon me for noticing that it all sounds *mighty* genocidal, whitey.

Belching out the sort of logic-defying, obfuscatory nonsense that has been a hallmark of their flailing attempts at discourse for generations now, Ciccariello-Maher's supporters claimed since there's no such thing as "white people," there could not possibly be anything such as "white genocide."

Mind you, these are the *same* dolts who openly gloat that "White America Is Dying," citing demographic trends they insist are inevitable.

So in other words, even though white people don't exist, it's a good thing that they're dying out, and you're a racist if you don't understand that.

Part of the reason so many people snort and guffaw at the notion of white genocide is that the term "genocide" itself is generally understood as something that happens quickly, openly, and violently. It is not perceived as something that happens gradually as a result of deliberate demographic meddling by the powers that be.

But according to Jewish lawyer Raphael Lemkin, who is credited with coining the term "genocide" after World War II:

> *Genocide does not necessarily mean the immediate destruction of a nation....It is intended to signify a coordinated plan of different actions aiming at the destruction of essential foundations of the life of national groups, with the aim of annihilating the groups themselves....The objectives of such a plan would be the disintegration of the political and social institutions, of culture, language, national feelings, religion....*

Proponents of the "white genocide" hypothesis claim that this is precisely what's happening in Western countries—and *only* Western countries—through loose immigration policies and nonstop voodoo propaganda about the moral turpitude of not only white people—who, again, don't really exist—but the very *notion* of whiteness.

They claim that the mass infusion of nonwhite populations into Europe and the United States—which has never been democratically approved of by any of the host populations and has instead been foisted upon them—violate this passage in 1948's United Nations Convention on the Prevention and Punishment of the Crime of Genocide:

*Deliberately inflicting on the group conditions of life cal-
culated to bring about its physical destruction in whole or
in part.*

The howling double standard—i.e., the fact that no
one is forcing Africa, Asia, or Israel to "diversify"
while cramming diversity into every majority-white
nation on earth—has led to Robert Whitaker's
famous phrase "Anti-racist is a code word for anti-
white."

Many point to an Austrian-Japanese man with the
unwieldy name of Richard von Coudenhove-
Kalergi as the original architect of white genocide.
Kalergi established the Paneuropean Union in 1923,
which many consider to be a precursor of the modern EU. In his 1925 book *Practical Idealism*, Kalergi
wrote:

*The man of the future will be of mixed race. Today's races
and classes will gradually disappear owing to the vanish-
ing of space, time, and prejudice. The Eurasian-Negroid
race of the future, similar in its appearance to the Ancient
Egyptians, will replace the diversity of peoples with a
diversity of individuals.*

According to Kalergi, who was not Jewish but was
apparently a rabid philo-Semite, Europe's Jews
would comprise an aristocratic "leader-nation" and

"spiritual nobility" for this harmoniously mongrelized new world order:

> No wonder that this people, that escaped Ghetto-Prison, developed into a spiritual nobility of Europe. Therefore a gracious Providence provided Europe with a new race of nobility by the Grace of Spirit....It is the Jewish Socialist leaders who want to redeem us with the highest self-denial from the original sin of capitalism, free people from injustice, violence and serfdom and change the liberated world into an earthly paradise.

History shows that those who seek to establish an "earthly paradise" usually wind up creating hell on Earth.

Modern leftists—since they're brainwashed zombies who'd rather eat a bullet than possibly admit that they're wrong—dismiss all talk of "white genocide" as paranoid conspiracy-mongering by "racists," an odious breed of exclusively white people who obviously need to be exterminated by all means necessary. While openly applauding the notion that whites are a "dying breed," they will gaslight the living *fuck* out of anyone who dares to *notice* that whites are a dying breed.

They will pretend not to notice that Bill Clinton said the "third great revolution of America" will be when the nation loses its "dominant European culture." They will gloss right over the fact that Joseph Biden said that whites becoming a minority in America is "the source of our strength." They're probably not even aware that the suspiciously twinkly-eyed failed vice-presidential candidate Tim Kaine recently said that "Caucasians...have to put ourselves into situations where we are the minority."

Ted Kennedy, the front man for the (cough) well-heeled globalist pro-immigration forces who pushed 1965's Hart-Celler Act, assured the nation that anyone who thought the new law would disrupt America's demographic balance was a paranoid loon.

From 1900 to 1960, America's white population was almost unchanged at around 90%. It is now teetering around 60%. American whites are expected to reach official minority status sometime around 2040.

It is estimated that in 1950, whites were around 28% of the global population. This quotient will dip below 10% by 2060.

Smarmy neo-commie twerps such as George Ciccariello-Maher openly cheer such demographic decline while denying that it's happening at all.

That's the behavior of either an insane person or an asshole—possibly both.

They'll continue laughing about the idea that it's all been planned. And even allowing that it might not have been planned at all—that it all may be some giant catastrophe caused by nothing more than utopian delusions rather than ethnic malice toward indigenous Europeans—it all seems to be unfolding exactly as planned anyway.

11

Dividing the White

A rally in Virginia on August 12, 2017 intended to "Unite the Right" ended in chaos and bloodshed. The way events unfolded suggests that the main battle plan for the powers that be in America has nothing to do with illusions such as "left" and "right"—nah, instead, their primary goal appears to be Dividing the White.

The rally was organized to protest the ongoing erasure of Confederate monuments throughout the South, specifically the Robert E. Lee statue in Charlottesville, VA. It was scheduled to launch at noon and featured speakers such as Richard Spencer, Mike Enoch, Matthew Heimbach, and Christopher Cantwell. A rather visually fetching poster advertising the rally shows Confederate statues silhouetted in the back as a squadron of Rebel-flag-waving Civil War soldiers, half with Pepe the

Frog's face, stand guard and defend the statues' honor. What appear to be some sort of German eagles fly above the soldiers. I'm not exactly up to date on my Nazi/eagle iconography, but it's fair to say the average brainwashed American observer could be forgiven if they thought the poster invoked Nazi and Confederate imagery. I don't think the organizers would try (or even wish) to deny it, either.

The rally's planners had jumped through every possible legal hoop to ensure that the rally would commence without a hitch. Once they were issued a permit, it was revoked by the coffee-bean-colored Wes Bellamy, Vice-Mayor of Charlottesville. Wes never seems to miss an opportunity to remind you of his blackness. Among the groups he has joined (and even led) include 100 Black Men of Central Virginia, Young Black Professional Network of Charlottesville, and Charlottesville/Albemarle Alliance of Black School Educators. In case you missed it, Wes Bellamy wants you to know he's black.

In tandem with his love of being black, Bellamy appears to hate white people. Over the years, Charlottesville, VA's current Vice-Mayor has posted the following gems on Twitter (republished unedited and uncorrected):

I always feel sorry for the black kid growing up around aloooooot of white people...

white chicks the devil

Lol funniest thing about being down south is seeing little white men and the look on their faces when they have to look up to you.

I hate seeing white people in Orangeburg

I DONT LIKE WHIT PEOPLE SO I HATE WHITE SNOW!!!!!

White women=Devil

Mind you, this is the guy who initially revoked a legal permit to hold a rally in Charlottesville on the premise that the attendees were hatemongers. I've searched and have been unable to find evidence of *any* of the scheduled speakers for the "Unite the Right" rally saying something quite on the Hate Level of "black women are the devil" or "I hate seeing black people in Arlington" or "I DON'T LIKE BLACK PEOPLE SO I HATE LICORICE!!!!!" Actually, I'd like to see any white politician in America who's said equivalent things and still has their job.

The point is that Wes Bellamy is vocally pro-black and anti-white, still has his job, and he tried to use government power to squash a pro-white rally. And I haven't seen anyone in the mainstream media even question whether there might be something even a tiny bit wrong with that scenario—some sort of, you know, insanely hypocritical double standard that might cause, or may even be *engineered* to cause, racial conflict rather than racial harmony.

To their credit, the ACLU stepped in and was able to reinstate the permit. On the eve of the rally, members of this coalition of neo-Confederates, white nationalists, Alt-Righters, and European traditionalists lit tiki torches and gathered beneath the Lee monument. Marchers chanted things such as "BLOOD AND SOIL" and "YOU WILL NOT REPLACE US." The most amusing footage from that night rally involves a trans dude who calls himself Emily Gorcenski freaking out that his side was severely outnumbered.

But his side—aided and abetted by the police, government officials, and nearly all of the media—would show up in full force the next day.

I did not attend the event, but from what I can piece together from firsthand accounts, this is roughly what happened:

On Saturday morning, rally attendees headed toward Lee Park, where the event was scheduled to launch at noon. En route, they were met by the usual ragtag patchwork coalition of bused-in masked white anarchists, shirtless local black males with homemade flamethrowers, and shrieking obese transgender wallabies from the nearby college. As is their habit, the Antifa types began screaming and taunting and poking. They allegedly spat at anyone suspected of being a "Nazi," also flinging urine, feces, rocks, and even cement-filled bottles at them.

Shortly before noon, police announced that a state of emergency had been declared and that the entire event therefore suddenly constituted an unlawful assembly. Pro-black Vice-Mayor Wes Bellamy's wish had been granted: There would be no pro-white rally in Charlottesville.

Everyone was ordered to leave Lee Park immediately or face arrest. Whether or not the police—or, more likely, the people who were pulling their strings—were aware of it, this is the tactical situation they were setting up: They were forcing a large crowd of easily identifiable pro-white activists to disperse straight into the maws of the BLM and Antifa fanatics who consider it their highest moral calling to bloody and kill any white person who publicly declares it's OK to be white.

I can see why the Black Lives Matter dudes, however knuckleheaded they are, would have problems with a pro-white rally. That's simply how phenotypical racial tribalism works. What's curious is the keening, unhinged hatred that the "anti-racist" whites have for their genetic cohorts who refuse to join them in their creepy, ethnomasochistic psychological self-cleansing rituals.

It's hard to argue against the contention that in the current climate, any white person who doesn't go out of their way to apologize for being a white person is Public Enemy Number One. What's sociologically fascinating is this intra-racial tribal war among what are called the goodwhites and the badwhites. In case you couldn't figure it out, the "goodwhites" are the ones that are constantly apologizing.

Shortly after being told that Lee Park was off-limits, police announced that the entire city of Charlottesville was an unlawful-assembly zone. The rally-goers were thus forbidden from holding smaller events in nearby parks. So as they dispersed, they were sent into the hands of bat-wielding local blacks, who persistently taunted them as they quietly tried walking to their cars.

I watched about twenty minutes of a livestream in Charlottesville where a lone white guy with a shaved head and sunglasses had a prolonged stand-off with dozens of local blacks and a smattering of communist white weirdlings who mostly stood back and let their more muscular black allies do most of the taunting. I also watched another livestream where Alt-Right types were walking away from the event were screamed at by blacks leaning out of passing cars. According to accounts, many of the blacks who roamed the streets of Charlottesville couldn't tell the difference between white nationalists and white anti-racists, so they harassed them all indiscriminately. This is funny to me for reasons that should be obvious.

What quickly became evident to me was that the authorities completely shut down an event where the organizers had a permit, but they didn't touch the roaming mobs of BLM and Antifa goons who hadn't bothered to obtain permits. Police allowed them to chant "WE HAVE REPLACED YOU" and "WE'RE HERE, WE'RE GAY, WE FIGHT THE KKK" despite that alleged order about all public assemblies being temporarily banned.

I watched the day's most infamous event, and the one that will be milked of every last drop for political purposes, right as it livestreamed—the car-plowing incident that allegedly caused the death of one woman and injuries to dozens of others. I watched a person die as it happened, and even though I wasn't there, it's a feeling you can't quite ever scrub from your mind. Plenty of evidence has emerged—and it will be suppressed—that before plowing into the crowd, murder suspect James Alex Fields, Jr.'s car had been repeatedly attacked by bat-wielding rioters.

Would this have happened if the event had gone on undisturbed and the police had provided adequate protection—like they're supposed to do when someone has a legal permit and has yet to break any laws?

Would it have happened if, after declaring the entire city a no-assembly zone, the police also forcibly dispersed the BLM and Antifa mobs rather than let them block streets throughout downtown?

Most importantly, would this have happened if the reigning *diktat* wasn't that the worst person on Earth, probably even worse than a murderer or a child molester, is a white person who says there's nothing wrong with being white?

Answers to those questions: no, no, and NO.

Naturally, the mainstream media is blaming "white supremacists," and ONLY "white supremacists," for the violence and bloodshed in Charlottesville. Then again, the media has been rancidly dishonest about leftist violence for years now. And politicians across the spectrum are singling out the pro-white folks for what happened. To his credit, Donald Trump blamed "all sides" for what happened, only to be called a Nazi.

I hate to break it to whomever thinks that politics in a multiracial society can ever be totally non-racial, but this eternally morphing movement known as "the right" will never be united while whites remain so divided. Y'all crackers need to work some shit out.

12

Where Are All the White Supremacists?

I woke up this morning, sneezed, and then suddenly every white person in the world was a "white supremacist."

And if they try to deny it, well, that only means they are white supremacists who lie about it.

Still flailing desperately like a half-crushed bug about its electoral defeat in November 2016, the modern left is tossing the term "white supremacist" at any suspected counterrevolutionaries with the same zealous abandon that Antifa chucks urine-filled bottles at old white ladies who wave American flags.

We are led to believe that race doesn't exist—which would imply that white people don't exist, either—but that through some sort of socially righteous prestidigitation, white people are easy to spot and must be scapegoated for all human, animal, and plant suffering across the universe from the dawn of time. And if you think that's a ridiculous burden to bear, that's only because you're a "white supremacist."

For about a quarter-century, I've been accused of being a "white supremacist" for no other apparent reason than the fact that I don't apologize for my skin color and don't feel one sliver of guilt for history. I've never felt the need to say that white people are the best on Earth, but this isn't what gets me labeled a white supremacist—it's my refusal to say they're the *worst* group on Earth.

I've often said I've never run across a true "Holocaust denier" in that sense that I've never seen anyone say Hitler loved Jews and that the Germans didn't kill any Heebs in World War II. Every "denier" I've ever seen only quibbles about numbers and methods of killing and how the Holocaust is used as a political weapon. So in essence, I deny the existence of Holocaust denial.

In the same sense, I'm not sure in my long and arduous research that I've ever encountered a "white supremacist," at least according to the official definition. According to Merriam-Webster, a white supremacist is:

> *a person who believes that the white race is inherently superior to other races and that white people should have control over people of other races*

Wikipedia defines "white supremacy" thusly:

> *a racist ideology based upon the belief that white people are superior in many ways to people of other races and that therefore white people should be dominant over other races.*

Of all the alleged "white supremacists" I've known—at that's at least enough to fill a small dinner theater for a musical tribute to Al Jolson—I'd estimate that only a slim quotient has even gone so far as to say that whites are superior to all others. And I can't recall a single one of them ever saying that "white people should have control over people of other races." At most, they just want to get the hell *away* from other races. Those would accurately be termed "white separatists" or "white nationalists." But the modern media/government/banking complex doesn't seem to care about accuracy nearly as much as they enjoy hunting white witches. These days, being called a "white supremacist" is only different from being called a witch in that they don't even bother dunking you in the river before declaring you guilty.

I covered this in my recent podcast interview with Jared Taylor, who identifies as a "race realist" and has repeatedly said that Asians are "objectively superior" to whites. Still, Wikipedia insists on calling him a "white supremacist"—on the same page that they note his comments about Asian superiority.

Exactly how much mental yoga does it take to call someone a white supremacist when they've clearly explained why they aren't?

And why is the word "supremacist" used almost entirely to smear white-identity groups and no others? A quick Google search yielded the following:

"white supremacist"...9,680,000 results
"jewish supremacist"...192,000 results
"black supremacist"...110,000 results
"asian supremacist"...2,670 results

Pardon me for noticing, but the term "God's chosen people" is one of the most baldly supremacist notions ever concocted. It takes supremacy all the way up to the *cosmic* plane. And at least over the past generation, I've witnessed far more Jewish, black, and Asian people than whites claiming to be members of the master race. For the most part, all these alleged "white supremacists" are simply sick of the constant defamation.

It's almost as if the people who lob the term "white supremacist" with impunity are either painfully stupid or deeply malicious. And despite the relentless gaslighting, one needn't be a paranoid schizophrenic to suspect there's an explicitly anti-white agenda underlying it all. Then again, even insinuating that anything could possibly be "anti-white" automatically gets you labeled a white supremacist.

Reality TV star Mike Rowe of *Dirty Jobs* notoriety was recently accused of supporting "white nationalism" because he didn't explicitly condemn Donald Trump's factually accurate comment that there was violence on "both sides" in Charlottesville. Rowe fired back that he felt no need to do the whole hairshirt-wearing "disavowal" tap dance because the very request to do so is "annoying."

Despite taking great pains to distance himself from white identity movements, Charles Murray has been smeared by the Southern Poverty Law Center as a "white nationalist." Perhaps people should start suing anyone who makes such an accusation, because in this climate, it's effectively an invitation to commit violence against someone. Such propaganda actually led to violence in Murray's case early in 2017.

When organizers for a group called Patriot Prayer—a group that does not mention race at all—attempted to hold a rally in San Francisco recently, Nancy Pelosi defamed them as "white nationalists" and others called them "white supremacists." Naturally, the rally was canceled as a result.

After the Charlottesville debacle, former Vice President Joe Biden said that Donald Trump has "emboldened white supremacists" by drawing a false moral equivalency "between neo-Nazis and Klansmen and those who would oppose their venom and hate."

Huh. All I got from what Trump said was a factually irrefutable statement that there was violence on both sides. Saying that one side dripped with venom while the other side was merely there innocently and nonviolently opposing venom-drippers is either dishonest or dumb.

A Twitter account called "Yes, You're Racist"—which is devoted to calling people "racist" and destroying their lives as a result—showed a picture of a man rallying with right-wingers in Charlottesville while wearing a shirt with an Arkansas Engineering emblem. The digital torch mob wound up targeting and harassing Kyle Quinn, who works at the University of Arkansas. It turns out that they were wrong—Quinn was not the man in the picture—but being wrong hardly seems to matter to fanatics.

When Bernie Sanders told a Latina woman that she should focus not only on her race, but on fighting Wall Street and corporate America, he was accused of "defending white supremacy."

Perhaps the most egregious example of this new White Scare happened in Boston shortly after the Charlottesville disaster. A "Boston Free Speech Rally" that attracted a few dozen attendees who bent over backwards and grabbed their ankles trying to distance themselves from "racism" and "white supremacy" were met with a crowd of 40,000 fanatics screaming about "Nazis." A *Boston Globe* reporter recalls the tragic question a counter-protester asked him:

Excuse me, where are the white supremacists?

They're all in your propaganda-addled brain, you fool. And they're hiding under your bed as you sleep.

13

Diagnosing "Passover Syndrome" Among White Liberals

There's something to be said for the almost universal leftist tendency to ignore unpleasant facts in favor of smearing their opponents as mentally ill. Not only is it far easier than constructing a coherent argument, it often works marvelously as a propaganda technique.

Therefore, I can't see these well-meaning Left Bank humanists complaining if I were to borrow their time-tested methods to describe a prominent mental disorder that currently runs rampant—although undiagnosed and untreated—among their own ilk.

I call this disorder "Passover Syndrome." Almost exclusively, it afflicts relatively affluent Caucasians and is characterized by an array of cognitive delusions that ultimately may prove dangerous for its sufferers and those around them.

Passover Syndrome's most prominent behavioral feature consists of whites projecting historical blame onto other whites and hoping that non-whites will see them as not-so-white for doing so. Just as the ancient Israelites smeared sacrificial lamb's blood over their doorways in order to escape the Angel of God's vengeance, these delusional Caucasians smear bright red anti-racist graffiti—or, in extreme cases, the literal blood of "rednecks" and any "right-wing white" who refuses to get with the program—over their doorways in the hope that when the Dark Angels finally come *en masse* seeking "justice," they won't accidentally notice that the people with the bright red anti-racist paint over their doorways also happen to be white.

What drives this syndrome is the delusion that collective historical ethnic guilt is a real thing rather than a pseudo-religious abstraction. Passover Syndrome's sufferers tend to believe that all whites, by dint of skin color alone, are indelibly stained with guilt for kazillions of historical atrocities and that their debt to nonwhites won't be repaid until the very concept of "whiteness" ceases to exist—if not white people themselves.

What's most curious about this syndrome is the delusion that by merely *acknowledging* this imagined historical debt, they are able to somehow *transfer* it onto other whites—the "unenlightened" ones who don't acknowledge it—without having to make any sacrifices or installment payments of their own. A consistent feature of Passover Syndrome is an eagerness to offer up a whole other group of whites as sacrificial collateral for their own perceived debt. It's fundamentally irrational and unethical to believe that one can atone for one's guilt, real or imagined, by transferring it onto a family member, yet this delusion is surprisingly strong among those afflicted with the disorder.

Indeed, guilt projection is one of Passover Syndrome's most consistent features. Although the malady almost solely attacks Caucasians in high-income brackets, sufferers tend to blame lower-class "rednecks" and "white trash" for slavery and its after effects. In truth, it's far more probable that affluent Caucasians are descended from slaveowners than are low-income whites, who are more likely to count indentured servants among their progenitors. This constant finger-pointing of others as "racists," all while exhibiting an unceasing obsession with racial matters, also strongly suggests projection.

Passover Syndrome is similar to homophobia in that its sufferers make a point at every turn of assuring you that they aren't racist, much as the homophobe feels a neurotic compulsion to constantly remind you he isn't gay. Passover Syndrome shares features with Stockholm Syndrome in that its sufferers mistake as benevolence the fact that those who have a perceived right to kill them still haven't killed them. This is often misinterpreted as tolerance and acceptance rather than, say, procrastination or lack of opportunity. Passover Syndrome also has many traits in common with oikophobia—the antonym to xenophobia, meaning a fear of the familiar and of one's surroundings—but since so many Westerners who dominate the social sciences are themselves afflicted with oikophobia, this grievous disorder has not yet been properly classified as a mental disease.

Self-deception is another common factor in Passover Syndrome. Sufferers identify with the "underclass," yet they never seem to come from it nor actually spend any meaningful time around its members. In many if not most cases, they live in far safer and whiter areas than the white "racists" do. Therefore, while they claim to intimately understand "racism," they rarely have experienced the sort of competition over jobs and resources that historically gives rise to ethnic conflict.

A common delusion among Passover Syndrome sufferers is that they represent the cusp of some bold revolutionary cultural vanguard rather than modern mainstream society itself. They seduce themselves into thinking they are rebels against an oppressively racist society, yet there is nothing dangerous or career-threatening in anything they say. In truth, to *disagree* with what they say is to court ostracism, assault, and possible legal action. So rather than being mavericks in the Nat Turner mold, their personalities more fit that of the obsequious and conformist House Negro who toes the party line with a wide, bucktoothed grin. They seem cognitively incapable of grasping the fact that their personalities are indeed so fundamentally conformist, they may have participated in lynch mobs a century ago.

In keeping with such conformist tendencies, they apprehend clearly that the "racist" is our society's new "nigger," and they want everyone to know, as loudly as they can manage without being arrested for disturbing the peace, that they're with the majority this time as far as hating niggers is concerned.

Despite the desire to conform, severe social maladjustment is always present in Passover Syndrome. Any sort of nonwhite group the world over would brand such personality types as evil, freakish tribal enemies. The fact that nonwhites appreciate and welcome their overtures does not mean they *respect* them. The truth is that nonwhite cultures don't tolerate traitors within their ranks to nearly the degree that supposedly ethnocentric whites do. Imagine a black person being able to make a career out of campaigning against black pride. Nonwhite cultures—to their credit—tend to view such individuals as sellouts, punks, and snitches.

A daily ritual among Passover Syndrome sufferers, as reflexive as washing their hands and brushing their teeth, is to smear an invisible layer of protective talismanic blackface on themselves. But until scientists develop full-body skin transplants, there's nothing they'll be able to do about it in practical terms. They're pretty much stuck being white. Most nonwhites still see them, above all else, as white. Passover Syndrome sufferers would realize this if they'd actually spent any time in jail or had ever lived in a mostly nonwhite neighborhood.

While they may compare themselves to abolitionist John Brown—who may or may not have been mentally ill or suicidal, but given the historical context, at least he was bravely nonconformist—their dangerously delusional behavior is more similar to that of Timothy "Grizzly Man" Treadwell, who spent several summers attempting to live harmoniously amid grizzly bears until one of them ate him.

Although they tend to consider themselves sophisticated, Passover Syndrome sufferers are fundamentally naïve. Fatally naïve. They encourage tribal
identity among nonwhites and forbid it among
whites, yet they fail to see how such a double standard works against any hope of eventual ethnic harmony. They fail to grasp that the day may never
come when their childlike fantasies come true and
people of all colors hold hands, sing protest songs,
and gently melt together into a non-threatening
shade of beige.

It is said that a conservative is a liberal who's been
mugged, but in its advanced stages, Passover Syndrome appears to be incurable. Witness the white
activist named Amanda Kijera who moved to Haiti
and suffered an all-night brutal rooftop raping at
the hands of one of her black "brothers," only to
blame it on "the white patriarchy," members of
whom were suspiciously absent during her assault.
Or observe the eagerness to excuse a recent anti-
white bloodbath by framing it within a context of
unsubstantiated allegations that the gunman, a
black man named Omar Thornton, had endured
racist jokes at work.

If a racial Doomsday ever comes in America, I
doubt that the nonwhite marauders will ever draw
fine distinctions between the "good" whites and
the "bad" ones. I lived a half-block off Hollywood

Boulevard during the 1992 L.A. riots, and I recall a member of rap group Boo-Yaa T.R.I.B.E. being quoted as saying that the rioters should quit looting South-Central L.A. and instead burn down Beverly Hills—home of the exact record executives who finance anti-white albums by ingrates such as Boo-Yaa T.R.I.B.E.

If a large-scale Day of Racial Reckoning ever comes, Passover Syndrome sufferers will find that when it comes to hating whites, nonwhites truly don't discriminate. Rather than the sweet scent of compassion, those with the disorder emit the rancid smell of fear, and there's nothing a bloodthirsty mob savors more than the smell of fear. If a real race war were ever to pop off in America, they'd be the first to perish.

The only mystery is which side would kill them first.

14

Why Does Hollywood Ignore White Slavery?

The Los Angeles Times has congratulated Hollywood for congratulating itself for awarding the Best Picture Oscar to *12 Years a Slave*. The gist of the article is that Tinseltown is *finally* taking "risks" and tackling "difficult subjects" such as black slavery. Why, it's as if *Roots, Django Unchained, Amistad, Lincoln,* and *Glory* had never been made! It's as if we aren't helpless baby seals who are constantly clubbed over the head with the long-dead (in America, at least) institution of black slavery everywhere we turn, whether in kindergarten classes, on TV, in public monuments, and even in subway cars.

Black actor Danny Glover has been laboring for years to produce a film that treats the black Haitian genocide of the French as a heroic act, but there's a still small voice inside me that says he won't make a squeak about the allegation that French indentured servants in Haiti were said to be treated worse than black slaves and were often beaten to death.

Anytime someone dares shine a positive light on Thomas Jefferson, one is heckled with the unproved allegation that he fathered children with a black slave. This was treated as fact in the 1995 film *Jefferson in Paris*. Yet I can't recall ever seeing a film that deals with the fact that in 1775, George Washington offered a reward for the capture and return of eight runaway white servants who'd escaped his clutches.

And for all the countless movies that have been made about black slavery in America—even old ones such as *Gone With the Wind* and *The Birth of a Nation* that are now considered blasphemous—I can't ever remember seeing a film about white slavery. And when I say "white slavery," I don't mean sex trafficking—I mean the literal enslavement of white Europeans who were transported against their will to both Africa and America.

The telling of history is largely an exercise in guilt transference. Public perceptions of good guys and bad guys are shaped as much by what is omitted as by what is taught.

There are two types of ignorant people: those who don't know, and those who know but choose to ignore. While nary a day goes by when our pink snouts aren't rubbed in black slavery and the Holocaust, I can't remember the last time the media made a peep about white slavery in the American colonies—nor even its more benign term, white indentured servitude. Then again, one can't forget—nor even remember—what you don't know about in the first place.

I can count at least one distant ancestor who was transported to the New World as an indentured servant. I've dealt with the white-hot topic of white slavery in my book *The Redneck Manifesto* and in a magazine article that was factually correct yet allegedly cost the magazine in question significant ad revenue from disgruntled White Slavery Deniers. And every time I've dared to raise the subject, I am shouted down, scoffed at, spat upon, pooh-poohed, and falsely accused of trying to say "Black slavery wasn't bad." My true motive is to say, "Hey, numskulls—you're missing the big picture and creating poisonous levels of misunderstanding and resentment." I'm only trying to show the similarities between white and black slavery, while others seem compelled to deny the similarities and focus exclusively on the differences. Interestingly, black people generally seem far more receptive to my humble mission. Then again, the

false narrative that white people have never suffered is usually peddled by white people who have
never suffered.

Why don't we see Hollywood films about white
slavery? Probably for the same reason we don't see
Hollywood films about communist atrocities, nor
any films that focus on the tens of millions of white
civilians who died in World War II.

Knowing my suggestions will be ignored, I will
stubbornly sally forth and suggest two possible
Hollywood adaptions of real-life white slavery. The
first would involve the Barbary Coast and the estimated million-plus white Christians who were kidnapped by African Muslims and forced to endure
hardships and torture that rival and may surpass
what black slaves in America experienced.

The second would be based on the book *White
Cargo*. One in a long series of books and essays that
have exhaustively documented this otherwise
whitewashed phenomenon, *White Cargo* goes into
great detail regarding the brutality of the white
slave trade to America and how English and Irish
adults and children were kidnapped, beaten, tor-
tured, and worked to death in the New World. For
a touch of personal pathos, the screenplay might
focus on the tale of a skeleton that was discovered
in a Maryland basement in 2003 "in a hole under

a pile of household waste." The remains are presumed to be those of a 16-year-old white so-called indentured servant who'd been worked to death and cast aside as white trash rather than given a proper burial. Let's see that poor soul's story up on the silver screen, Mr. Weinstein.

I won't hold my breath. For now, the film industry's moguls seem content to keep hammering down the nail that sticks up the most. It is a myopic and divisive strategy, yet division probably best serves their interests. The maniacal fixation on black slavery and the concomitant denial of white slavery is used both as a truncheon to instill universal white guilt and a crutch to explain away all black failure. To even acknowledge that white slavery happened would disrupt The Narrative, and once The Narrative is even slightly rewritten, the whole screenplay falls apart. And that would be the last thing Hollywood wants.

15

White Slavery Denial

The currently approved conceptual framework for American race relations dictates that whites—all of them, simply by dint of being white—are oppressors. Any deviation from this rigid script, no matter how deeply rooted in fact, must be immediately squashed like a blood-engorged tick.

We are taught that black academic and financial underperformance—as well as black over-performance in crime—are the direct result of slavery's horrid legacy. There are to be no other possible explanations. To note the hugely embarrassing fact that American blacks live far longer and under vastly superior economic conditions in America than they do in any majority-black nation on Earth may be factual, but it is RACIST because it undermines the ironclad Guilt Narrative that must never be questioned.

Here are some facts that The Script demands you ignore:

1) Even at the peak of American slavery, only a tiny percentage of American whites—about 1.5%—owned slaves.

2) Leading up to the Civil War, a vastly higher quotient of whites had worked as indentured servants and convict laborers than had ever owned slaves. Most historians, regardless of their political orientation, agree that anywhere from half to two-thirds of whites who came to the American colonies arrived in bondage. The fact that the vast majority of whites existed in a state closer to slavery than to slave ownership is something resolutely ignored in the modern retelling of history.

3) Documents from the era show that so-called white "indentured servants" were often referred to as "slaves" rather than "servants."

4) These "servants" did not always enter into voluntary contracts. There is overwhelming evidence that many of them were kidnapped by organized criminal rings and sent to work on American plantations. It is possible that as many, if not more, whites than blacks were brought involuntarily to the colonies.

5) The middle-passage death rates for these "servants" were comparable to that of blacks on slave ships from Africa to the New World.

6) Indentured servants were whipped and beaten, sometimes to death. When they escaped, ads were placed for their capture.

7) They lived under conditions so brutal that an estimated half of them died before their seven-year term of indenture expired.

Since the currently enforced narrative is based far more on an attempt to quarantine historical guilt among whites than it is a sober assessment of the facts, the typical response to any discussion about white slavery is emotional rather than logical.

Ninety-nine percent of the time, "rebuttals" consist of nothing more than ad-hominem attacks, straw men, and appeals to motive. I often get accused of trying to "justify" slavery or of trying to argue that two wrongs make a right. When I counter that I'm arguing that two wrongs make two wrongs—and that I wonder why the sole focus is on *one* wrong rather than all of them—I am accused of being a racist liar.

Most frustratingly, I'm falsely accused of saying that white slaves had it worse than black slaves.

No, actually, in *The Redneck Manifesto*, I was merely *quoting* people who alleged as much:

> *Howard Zinn states that "white indentured servants were often treated as badly as black slaves." Eugene Genovese claims that "In the South and in the Caribbean, the treatment meted out to white indentured servants had rivaled and often exceeded in brutality that meted out to black slaves...."*

OK, well, obviously those were neo-Nazi, Holocaust-denying, minority-lynching, right-wing KKK lunatics saying that, right? No—both Zinn and Genovese were Marxists.

The book also quotes early observers saying much the same thing:

> *A colonial observer of Virginia convict laborers said, "I never see such pasels of pore Raches in my Life...they are used no Bater than so many negro Slaves." A 1777 screed protesting the indenture racket claimed that a white servant's body was "as absolutely subjected as the body or person of a Negro, man or woman, who is sold as a legal Slave." In the 1820s, Karl Anton Postl commented that non-slaveowning whites "are not treated better than the slaves themselves....A 1641 law provided for all disobedient servants to have their skin branded, regardless of its color. A 1652 law in Providence and Warwicke (later Rhode Island) mentions "blacke mankind or white" servants. A*

1683 Pennsylvania law contains the phrase "no Servant White or Black.

But rather than even attempting to dispute any of this, critics merely call me a white supremacist and think they've won. That's truly how stupid they are. Or dishonest. Or stupidly dishonest and dishonestly stupid.

In May 2016 I was alerted by about a half-dozen friends to a story circulating about the "Myth of the 'Irish slaves'" and how it was based on "a purposeful lie" spread by "Neo-Nazis, White Nationalists, Neo-Confederates, and even Holocaust deniers." If that sounds like the frothy, methinks-the-lady-doth-protest-too-much vituperations of a Southern Poverty Law Center press release, that's exactly what it was. The article features an interview with a certain Liam Hogan—who is nothing more than an Irish librarian—in a frantic attempt to "debunk" this "myth."

Hogan's "refutation" consists of little more than character smears. When he wades shallowly into the factual realm, it's only to prove that some dumb meme somewhere misidentified a picture of bedraggled white children as white Irish slaves. But by that reasoning, since rumors of human soap and human lampshades were proved to be false, *that* whole story falls apart...right? Otherwise, there is absolutely no refutation of the reams of documented evidence that not only did white slaves exist, they were often *called* slaves back then. Again, from *The Redneck Manifesto*:

> *During a 1659 Parliamentary debate on the white-servant trade to the colonies, legislators used the word "slaves" rather than "servants." A Virginia law of 1705 mentions the "care of all Christian slaves," Christian being a contemporary euphemism for European.*

In my long and checkered life I've often found that people who make huge public displays of virtue-signaling and moralistic grandstanding are often engaging in projection. In an article called "'Irish slaves': the convenient myth," Hogan writes:

> *The conflation of indentured servitude with chattel slavery in the 'Irish slaves' narrative whitewashes history in the service of Irish nationalist and white supremacist causes.*

OK, two can play at that game. How's this sound?

> *The media and academic blackout regarding white indentured servitude and convict labor—which were often referred to simply as "slavery" by contemporaries—whitewashes history in the service of a pro-black, pro-Jewish, anti-white cause.*

Hogan also drags the Ferguson, MO riots into it:

Its resurgence in the wake of Ferguson reflects many Americans' denial of the entrenched racism still prevalent in their society.

So I'll drag Ferguson out of it:

The fact that white slavery deniers are using Ferguson to somehow dispel white slavery as a "myth" shows how desperate and intellectually bankrupt they've become in their attempt to quarantine historical guilt solely among non-Jewish whites.

But to white slavery deniers such as Liam Hogan and the SPLC, to even dare drawing analogies between black slavery and white indentured servitude is to peddle "false equivalencies"—possibly because to do so renders the idea of universal white guilt as undeniably false. So it's not a case of me *denying* guilt—it's a case of others *falsely imputing* it.

Since so much of leftist "argumentation" these days consists of guilt by association, the SPLC and Hogan ignore the Marxist and centrist historians who agree that white slavery was rampant and brutal. Instead, they go straight for the jugular of anyone they can dismiss as a white supremacist Nazi Holocaust-denier.

Enter one Michael A. Hoffman II, easily one of the most interesting alternative historians on Earth, even though Wikipedia's dutiful social-justice termites have pegged him mainly as a "Holocaust denier and conspiracy theorist." Along with over a hundred other sources, I cited Hoffman's book *They Were White and They Were Slaves* several times in *The Redneck Manifesto*. Wikipedia mentions the book, but in true fashion it doesn't bother to note its staggering reams of documentation from primary sources—instead, it heads straight into a critic's description of Hoffman as a "racist."

Although Hogan's "Irish slaves myth" story was spread far and wide on several sites, no one bothered to contact the alleged primary myth-maker.

The following Q&A was conducted with Michael A. Hoffman II via email.

* * * * * * * * * * *

Jim Goad: Throughout his purported "debunking," Hogan floats the idea that white indentured servitude and black slavery were so different as to be incomparable. Why is he wrong?
Michael A. Hoffman II: White enslavement has a long history in Britain and Scandinavia. Mr. Hogan, like so many writers on this subject who conform to the Establishment line, overlooks several points and has a naive faith in the white ruling class of Britain.

The conforming authors don't take into account that the study of white enslavement has been impeded over the centuries by two facts missing from their own studies and critiques. First, white enslavement carried with it a hereditary taint. As I demonstrate in my book, this extends back to the Vikings who looked on Scandinavian "thralls" and those born into "thralldom" as carrying a hereditary defect in part because their enslavement was hereditary. Something akin to this was operating in Anglo-Saxon England under the category of villeinage. The daughter of a villein could not be married without buying her way out of villeinage. The test of a young English woman's status in early medieval England—whether she was slave or free—was decided by whether or not the local lord had control over her body, as all masters have over their slaves. Under English law, a villein woman was one who could not be married until she first offered the custom of the country as it was known, the "ransom of blood for *merchet*" (i.e., until she first submitted to sexual intercourse with the lord, prior to her marriage).

Both in early Britain and Scandinavia and much later in the sugar plantations of the West Indies and the tobacco plantations of America (before cotton became king), British-American whites whose parents or relatives had been enslaved, or who themselves had escaped it, or bought their way out (as did some black people), were exceedingly reticent to identify as former white slaves or as their progeny. "Servant" was a far more attractive category, and we see identifications with this status and less so with outright enslavement due to the stigma.

Hogan has a pictorial display allegedly confuting my thesis in which he displays a photograph of what appear to be mixed-race people in the West Indies who are Barbados residents circa 1908, and he is incredulous that no Irish white "redlegs" are in the photo or named as such. We know from primary source materials that white slaves worked alongside blacks in the West Indies and that the word "redleg" was applied to them by their darker coworkers because of the tendency of the white slaves to sunburn. Whether or not their descendants stayed on the island to pose for a camera nearly 300 years later is a flimsy device for casting doubt on a historical epoch. Limiting oneself to the search for Irish surnames is an even more egregious error because it excludes the search for traces of the English Protestants who were transported as slaves to those islands in the 17th and early 18th century.

Hogan and company also support the notion that white bondage was mostly carried out within a framework of law. Here they are swallowing the propaganda of the white ruling class who were permitting the mass kidnapping of white children off the streets of port cities such as London and Glasgow for shipment to America under no indentures whatsoever, or under forged indentures, or as criminalized paupers and "rogues." Upon arrival these youth were often put to work clearing forests and draining swamps. They were regularly assaulted, illfed, and worked to death. Britain had a surfeit of poor white youth who represented a potential for a French-Revolutionary type of insurrection in the cities. The aristocracy was only too glad to be rid of them, and I draw my evidence for this from state papers and contemporary letters and eyewitness accounts.

Hogan accepts the official tale of the slavers themselves, as they obscured their monstrous crime against their own people. So for him, there is no mass "*kid-nabbing*" (as it was first termed). He is blind to the fact that to facilitate white bondage under penal enslavement, the British ruling class contrived laws such as the Waltham Black Act, which made simple misdemeanors (stealing lace, breaking down an aristocrat's fish pond, poaching deer) into felonies punishable by "transportation for life into the colonies." In the 17th century the tens of thousands of prisoners these laws netted were not sent to slavery in British America and the West Indies on indentures. They were sold at the ports on arrival. As prisoners they had no rights. Diaries, letters, and eyewitness accounts give testimony to their horrible mistreatment and slave labor. Mr. Hogan won't call these wretches "slaves," even though they were clearly handled like chattel (cattle).

It seems that a powerful lobby has decided that black folk have a proprietary relationship with the word slave. "You blacks are *the* slave race," they are told by their liberal white alleged "allies." If this designation is false, however, then it constitutes an act of psychological crippling. The history of the white race is in many respects synonymous with the long history of enslavement, and if blacks have a copyright on the word "slave," someone should tell that to the Slavic people, who for generations were targets of Viking slave raids and from whom the word "slave" is derived.

The weakness of Mr. Hogan's assertions can be found in his gullible acceptance of the party line of the white ruling class with regard to their white-wash of their role in white enslavement. The white ruling class is excoriated with contempt by the left when they minimize crimes of the British aristocracy and capitalists against people of color, but Mr. Hogan will believe them implicitly when they aver that white bondage was operated within a legal framework, and it only involved "servants."

The kidnapping of poor whites has precedence in Britain. It does not have a legal basis *per se*, but it has color of law and we find it in the systematic mass kidnapping of British people for maritime slavery aboard ship for the Royal Navy. I can anticipate the objection: The bondage was for a determinate period of time. Officially, yes. An Englishmen was kidnapped of the streets and country lanes of Britain with the connivance of the judiciary and conscripted for a period of years, but in actuality these determinate number of years was not worth the ink that had been used to write the paper, when it so happened that the victim of abduction was returning home from a five- or seven-year compulsory voyage. He saw the blessed shore of England at long last, prayed that his wife had not run off and that his children and parents still lived, and then a few miles from shore, another man-of-war sailed up to his vessel, boarded it at sea with a press gang, and kidnapped him again for another multi-year abduction. This could happen two or three times. The kidnapped sailor could be gone from Britain ten, fifteen, or twenty years and killed or severely injured during that time. I doubt Mr. Hogan would confer upon this naval slave that title because if the slave survived his ordeal he eventually went home. He had been a slave for a time, and to quibble over it is to do a grave disservice to the memory of tens of thousands of Royal Navy slaves. Impressment was one of the rotten roots, along with villeinage, that created a precedent for an institutional framework for white slavery concealed under cover of "indenture" or some other deceptive and cosmetic rubric.

In this passage, Hogan essentially accuses you and others of lying: "The inclination to describe these different forms of servitude using the umbrella term 'slavery' is a wilful [sic] misuse of language." Didn't contemporary legal documents often refer to alleged "indentured servants" as "slaves"?

The truth was in the writings of the white slaves themselves who referred to themselves as such, and eyewitnesses to their plight who wrote accounts of what they saw. This is in my book *They Were White and They Were Slaves.*

As for willful misuse of language, I suppose I should apologize for defying the Establishment-imposed monopoly on how the word "slave" is to be employed, but I cannot, because like all monopolies this one is a form of restraint, enforced by thought cops indifferent to truths that violate the whole foundation of their monopoly on history and white self-image.

Hogan claims your book deceptively uses "selective quotations taken from nearly 200 different secondary sources," that your motive is "to deny reparations for slavery in America," and that your "denial has a pro-slavery

ideological lineage."
One usually can discern that something is defective about an argument when it is *ad hominem*, and we discover this ill omen in Mr. Hogan's resort to Pavlovian incentives for stigmatizing a writer with pejoratives calculated to cue an intended audience of partisans that here is someone to despise and dismiss. If he's writing mainly for the benefit of Mark Potok and members of the new religion of Multiculturalism and Diversity, then he's in luck. If he seeks a wider audience, however, then I don't see how such tactics help to make his case.

The idea of paying reparations to any aggrieved racial or ethnic group is something with no appeal to me. It devolves into one-upmanship in the game of guilt imposition. Even in the matter of the Irish Catholic slaves, the focus is too narrow, and the subtext is one that excludes English Protestant slaves, since the Irish narrative is too often beholden to a vision of near-perpetual victimization by the English, which excludes the reality that a vicious white ruling class in London has seldom had any compunctions against betraying and enslaving their own white English yeomanry.

Do the English pay reparations to the Irish for what Oliver Cromwell did in transporting Irish slaves to the West Indies? Do the Catholics pay reparations for the pro-Catholic Stuart King Charles II for having shipped criminalized and enslaved English Protestants to the West Indies? A world full of victims demanding payment is a definition of a madhouse, not a civilization. The reparations process is very often politicized, with war victors or the plutocracy with the most bloat apportioning the guilt and assigning the victim status.

As a revisionist historian, I wrote *They Were White and They Were Slaves* for the astonishing reason (to some observers) that it was a chronicle that had not been adequately addressed and thus was pure gold from the standpoint of historical rediscovery. My "sin" is to have detailed the history without regard to the idol of political correctness. My book is good news for black people: You are not inferior; you were not the only race or the main race in chattel bondage.

In an earlier email you wrote to me: "the work of my opponents (at least Hogan that is; the distaff side of the trio today admitted to me that she has not read my book), is so blundering (at least what I have read so far) as to actually add ammunition to my thesis." How so?
Hogan, Matthew Reilly, and Laura McAtackney make the case for one of the assertions in my book. They write:

"If a white servant assaulted another servant or a slave, it was treated as a misdemeanor and they were fined. *If they assaulted their master they were whipped.* Their indenture was legal property therefore a servant's remaining time could be left in wills, traded for commodities and sold. Since one's labor is inseparable from one's person, this meant indentured servants in Barbados were treated as a sort of commodity. The distinction between voluntary and involuntary indentured servitude is also important, but all too often serves as justification for the existence of 'white slavery.' It is true that some Europeans, particularly prisoners of war or political prisoners, were sent to places like Barbados against their will and without a predetermined period of servitude. *However, upon arrival, those without contracts were, by law, required to serve the master who purchased their labor for a limited number of years, depending on their age. It is also true that many servants didn't live to see the end of their period of servitude due to brutal treatment and unsparing work regimens,* but while under the conditions of servitude, they were subject to the same laws that governed European servants, not enslaved Africans." (End quote; emphasis supplied).

Apart from the risible fiction that all white bondage was "indentured" and for a "predetermined period" and therefore all of it was scrupulously governed by some kind of "European servant" legislation and jurisprudence, Hogan, Reilly, and McAtackney concede that "many" whites in bondage suffered "brutal treatment and unsparing work regimens" which proved lethal.

Even they admit that many whites were sent into bondage in Barbados and then worked to death. This is not slavery and it cannot be designated chattel slavery? By what sufficiently dainty term do we describe it? The death of many "servants" was by accident? Were their masters prosecuted and executed for this? What sort of human being who is beaten and worked to death is undeserving of the name "slave"?

Notice as well the knee-jerk assumption the three critics of white slave history exhibit: They expect us to believe that in every case where a white person in bondage is whipped, it was because "they assaulted their master." How do they know this? Imagine the outcry if someone made such a characterization about the whipping of blacks in bondage—that the flogging was always their fault?

How is the experience of whites in servitude, who were at the mercy of masters of all types, reducible to the notion that no master ever unjustly lashed an un-free white person? This myth presupposes that whites were never whipped due to having tried to run away, or because they were too sick to work, or they refused the master's sexual advances. By some miracle, the human predicament by which nonwhites in bondage unjustly found themselves on the receiving end of a lash is not shared by whites in bondage. Here we observe the subhuman status of whites in servitude as we demarcate the dimensions of the distortion: They died as slaves yet must not be called slaves; unlike black human beings who experienced servitude and were unconscionably whipped, whites who were whipped almost always deserved it.

Isn't it true that several historians who can in no way be smeared as "holocaust deniers" or "white suprema-cists" essentially agree that white slavery existed in the colonies? In my research for The Redneck Manifesto, *I found historians across the political spectrum essentially agreeing with the historical facts you raise in your research.*

The cumulative evidence of A. Roger Ekirch in *Bound for America* (1990) is conclusive, though he employs euphemisms for white enslavement. He certainly does not fit the hysteric's categories of "denier" or "supremacist." Oscar and Mary Handlin openly refer to whites in servitude in the seventeenth century as "slaves. " See "Origins of the Southern Labor System" in *William and Mary Quarterly*, April, 1950. Personally, I rely mainly on testimony of the white slaves themselves, their own writings and pleadings and those persons high and low who encountered them and wrote of them.

So much of Hogan's alleged "debunking" simply employs the fallacies of argumentum ad hominem *and appeal to motive. But since he called your motives into question, what might be someone's motive in denying the well-documented history of white slavery?*

In my book I give examples of white British aristocrats speeding in their carriages to abolitionist meetings where the plight of blacks in America was decried, heedless of white children by the side of the road who had finished toiling 16 hours, half-naked in a mine; or having their arms and legs mutilated in the factory machinery of the early Industrial Revolution whose owners, such as Josiah Wedgewood, and the famous poet and mine owner Lord Byron, considered poor British whites entirely expendable.

Charles Dickens, who had been a child laborer in a chemical factory, termed this callous hypocrisy "telescopic philanthropy." The white elite of Britain had the apparition of black enslavement constantly before their eyes, even though it was thousands of miles away, while they were oblivious to the English boys who were sold to chimney sweeps and who sometimes burned and suffocated to death in the chimneys of the magnificent mansions of the abolitionists. Almost no one was paying attention to their agony. It's supposed to be naughty of me to refer to child labor in the factories, mines, and chimneys of Britain as white slavery. I do not know what else to term girls and boys stripped virtually naked toiling side-by-side in a mine for 16 hours stunted and blackened, or a factory, where they often were seriously injured or killed, because if they didn't undertake this labor they would starve to death. They went to their labor before dawn and ceased their labors after dark.

Most of your readers are familiar with white self-hatred and this perverse loathing, coupled with the legacy of the betrayal of the masses of white paupers and laborers in Britain by their rulers, has created the current situation of ruinous psychological and spiritual alienation that would seem to desire demographic extinction of their own seed.

16

The Other White Meat

Despite the ceaseless yippety-yap one hears about "white privilege," the glaringly obvious privilege currently denied to white Americans is the privilege to feel OK about their racial identity. Unless you wear your skin as if it were a guilt-laden hairshirt, and unless you frame white history as nothing more than one giant unpardonable sin against humanity, you will be hounded and mocked and derided and demonized. The way things stand, there is no such thing as a "self-hating white person." Instead, those are known as the "good" whites. The remaining whites—the ones who either take pride in their racial identity or really don't give a fig about it either way—are witches in the process of being rounded up and burned at the stake.

When I was younger and more easily manipulated by propaganda, I was naïve enough to think that being against "racism" meant that *everyone* should be required to lay down their tribal spears and join one big happy drum circle. I never expected that the more that white people willingly discarded their group identity, the more that other groups would double down on their own. I didn't think every concession would only bring demands for more concessions. But over time I wised up and realized it was all a sly game of ethnic musical chairs that ultimately had white people falling on their asses.

White pride is the only sort of ethnic identity whose expression is all but legally forbidden. It's certainly the biggest cultural sin you can currently commit.

This was all made howlingly clear in 2015 after a Colorado barbecue joint announced that it had designated June 11 as a "White Appreciation Day" during which a 10% discount would be offered to all white customers.

The barbecue joint in question bears the decidedly déclassé name of "Rubbin' Buttz" and is located in the tiny burg of Milliken, Colorado, which somehow manages to simultaneously be 73.89% white and 40.75% "Hispanic or Latino." The town is less than one third of one percent black, which is a heinous affront to black Americans' grand and noble tradition of spit-roasting pigs with great aplomb. And let's temporarily banish from our minds the undeniable fact that serving pork—AKA "the other white meat"—is inherently anti-Semitic and Islamophobic. Please try to understand that articles of this length only permit me to deal with so much imaginary hatred at a time.

The kicker here is that Rubbin' Buttz's co-owners are Hispanic rather than Anglo. Edgar Antillon's parents were born in Mexico. His partner Miguel Jimenez is also of Mexican descent. Antillon told a reporter that his idea for "White Appreciation Day" came from a discussion he had with Jimenez. He says the idea began as a "joke" but morphed into something more serious:

> We have a whole month for Black History month, we have a whole month for Hispanic heritage month, so we thought the least we could do was offer one day for white people.

Of course this did not sit well, especially with the millions of "good" white people on social media. The standard retort was that EVERY day is supposedly "White Appreciation Day" and our culture is unfairly rigged to favor whites above all other groups, and if you can't see that, you must be some toothless racist Neanderthal redneck whose demographic demise and eventual extinction is the only thing worth celebrating here.

Antillon even claims he was forced to temporarily evacuate the restaurant after receiving a bomb threat. We live in a creepy and insane era where people make bomb threats in the name of tolerance.

For those who still want to drag out the "white privilege" canard, yes, on average, white Americans enjoy a higher per-capita income than blacks and Hispanics. But they suffer a lower per-capita income than Asians and Jews. So it would seem that our economic system is more designed to reward mean group intelligence rather than white skin.

But Asians, Jews, blacks, and Hispanics are all encouraged to fairly *bask* in their ethnic identity. Whites are not. And when whites inevitably become an American minority—a demographic fact that seems to make many nonwhites and all of the "good" whites absolutely giddy—will they still be denied the privilege of acting in collective self-interest without being ostracized and demonized?

It seems likely, but it may not matter. By then, survival may seem more urgent than avoiding disapproval. If the modern American situation becomes akin to what happened after the Haitian Revolution or after Rhodesia became Zimbabwe, white meat may start being hunted for sport. And that may cause white people to rapidly start "appreciating" themselves whether others like it or not.

In the face of the backlash and alleged bomb threat, Rubbin' Buttz's owners said that they did not plan to abandon White Appreciation Day, but they will instead extend their 10% discount to everyone. In a desperate gesture of appeasement, they even began trotting out MLK and Anne Frank quotes on their Facebook page.

The fact that Antillon and Jimenez are Hispanic probably means that their restaurant will survive the backlash. It's currently far less scandalous to be pro-white if you're not actually white. But recently in New Jersey, a white deli owner was run out of business after he put up a "white history month" sign in his store window. His sin, but of course, was simultaneously being white and being OK with it. These days, that's as blasphemous as parading a pork chop through the dusty streets of Mecca.

17

The Greatest Anti-White Boxer of All Time

Muhammad Ali, widely regarded as the world's most famous man, died in June 2016 at age 74. Born Cassius Marcellus Clay, he was a titan both as a boxer and a provocateur.

Because we live in an era much weaker and more sensitive than it was during Ali's prime, his death is being eulogized with the sort of solemn, sancti-mony-addled, weak-tea, low-T, hagiographic twad-dle we've come to expect from neutered zombie bloggers on antidepressants. Just as mainstream history has Photoshopped all the warts off Nelson Mandela and MLK, Ali is now strictly framed as an inspirational figure who "spoke out against racism." (Certainly they don't mean the time he condemned interracial sex before a cheering crowd of Klans-men?)

The sad truth is that by shellacking history with a paintbrush soaked in modern pieties, they're suppressing how hilariously *insensitive* Ali was. For example, after being forced into an impromptu photo session with The Beatles in 1964, he reportedly turned to an associate and asked, "So who were those little faggots?"

Mere weeks later, he announced that he was changing his "slave name" of Cassius Marcellus Clay to Muhammad Ali at the behest of Elijah Muhammad, leader of the Nation of Islam. For years, Ali would be used as a completely hoodwinked and manipulated and bamboozled puppet of the NOI and its ditzy theories about Yakub and the Mother Plane.

But sad to say, despite their well-deserved reputation as tremendous athletes and sparkling entertainers, many American blacks have an unfortunate tendency to do dopey things when attempting to "reclaim" their lost heritage. For example, when they renounce Christianity in favor of Islam, they are merely trading one group of their former slave masters for another. Likewise, the original Cassius Marcellus Clay—after whom the boxer was named—was a white *anti-slavery* crusader who fought with the Union in the Civil War, whereas Muhammad Ali of Egypt was a warlord whose army *enslaved* the Sudanese.

From 1964 to 1980, Clay/Ali gifted the world with a string of spectacularly insensitive comments that would get any modern white man socially exiled to Pluto for daring to utter their equivalent:

> *"Integration is wrong. The white people don't want integration. I don't believe in forcing it...."*
> —*1964 interview with the Louisville Courier-Journal*

> *"The white man want me hugging on a white woman, or endorsing some whiskey, or some skin bleach, lightening the skin when I'm promoting black as best."*
> —*1966 interview with Sports Illustrated*

> *"My enemies are white people, not Viet Congs or Chinese or Japanese."*
> —*1967 interview regarding the draft*

> *"All Jews and gentiles are devils....Blacks are no devils....Everything black people doing wrong comes from the white people—drinking, smoking, prostitution, homosexuality, stealing, gambling—it all comes from (the white people)."*
> —*1969 interview with David Frost*

> *"Every intelligent person wants his child to look like him. I'm sad because I [don't] want to blot out my race and lose my beautiful identity? Chinese love Chinese—they love their little slanted-eyed, pretty brown-skinned babies. Pakistanis love their culture. Jewish people love their culture. Lotta Catholics don't wanna marry nothing but*

Catholics, they want their religion to stay the same. Who wanna spot up yourself and kill your race? You a hater of your people if you don't want to stay who you are."
—*1971 BBC interview with the portentously named Michael Parkinson*

"*A black man should be killed if he's messing with a white woman. And white men have always done that....And not just white men—black men, too. We will kill you, and the brothers who don't kill you will get their behinds whipped and probably get killed themselves if they let it happen and don't do nothin' about it."*
—*1975 interview with Playboy*

"*You know the entire power structure is Zionist. They control America; they control the world."*
—*1980 interview with India Today*

Ali relentlessly taunted other black boxers, calling them "Uncle Toms" and "gorillas." He once said that while clinching white boxers, he'd whisper in their ears that the Black Panthers knew where they lived and were going to burn their house down. He also reportedly lied in a 1975 autobiography when claiming that being refused service at a white restaurant caused him to toss his 1960 Olympics Gold Medal in the Ohio River. According to Ali's friend Bundini Brown, "Honkies sure bought into that one!"

Although Ali's indomitable ego fueled his ascen-dancy, it would later prove to be his undoing. He continued stubbornly fighting long after he'd lost his magic, and his 1980 battering at the hands of Larry Holmes was so lopsided, Holmes—a lifelong Ali fan—reportedly cried after the fight out of guilt. In 1984 Ali was diagnosed with what is now called Parkinson's disease. It was a grim prolonged public spectacle to view the once indomitably brash heavyweight champion reduced to a jittering mess whose condition was so familiar that comedian Greg Giraldo once joked to Pamela Anderson, "You've caused me to spill more seed than Muham-mad Ali at a bird feeder."

Since the 1960s are still remembered as the time when everything changed for the better rather than started falling apart, the reigning modern historians have recast Ali as a man of peace and healing and love and one-worldsmanship rather than the fear-less master of physical and psychological cruelty that he was.

Two of my favorite Ali quotes—besides "So who were those little faggots?," which will never be topped—touch upon one of the most unspeakable topics in this modern "conversation" about race which we're all supposed to be having but are simultaneously forbidden from even *beginning* to have. The topic is whether blacks, for all the oppression and brutality they allegedly endure in America, have it worse in Africa.

At the 1960 Rome Olympics, Ali told a reporter:

"To me, the U.S.A. is still the best country in the world, counting yours. It may be hard to eat sometimes, but anyhow I ain't fighting alligators and living in a mud hut."

After Ali spent months training in Zaire to fight George Foreman, a reporter asked him his impressions of Africa. Ali's response proves that although his IQ was twice tested at 78, he was a genius at making pithy rejoinders:

"Thank God my granddaddy got on that boat."

18

Nonwhites Can't Be Racist Cuz My Teacher Told Me So

There were audible sounds of indigestion online recently at the discovery of a textbook called *Is Everyone Really Equal?: An Introduction to Key Concepts in Social Justice Education*. The book is intended for all students of high school age and above. From a cursory glance of the book's advertising materials, it appears to be roughly as full of shit as its title would imply.

At issue recently was this specific passage:

> *There is no such thing as reverse racism or reverse sexism (or the reverse of any form of oppression). While women can be just as prejudiced as men, women cannot be "just as sexist as men" because they do not hold political, economic, and institutional power.*

Some would agree that there is indeed no such thing as "reverse racism," but they'd argue so for different reasons than the authors. They'd say racism is racism no matter who's practicing it. Unlike the authors of *Is Everyone Really Equal?*, at least they're being consistent.

But sensible citizens such as you and I realize that the voodoo term "racism" is purely a social construct and thus has no innate meaning. That's why different groups are always fighting one another to define it. The ability to define words is the root of cultural power. In my lifetime, the word's definition has expanded with the ravenousness of a malignant tumor. Nowadays, everything white is racist. Even pointing that out is racist. And it's racist of me for making fun of the fact that pointing this out is racist. And every word I keep saying from hereon out merely compounds the racism.

Will this tired conga beat never end? "Nonwhites cannot be racist" is a transparently nonsensical statement. It's a freeze-dried and vacuum-sealed bag of pure bullshit, one of those innately fraudulent Newspeak mantras that bother me more every time I hear them—you know, obvious lies such as "alcoholism is a disease," "rape has nothing to do with sex," and "race doesn't exist, but racism is rampant." It's an idea that makes no sense, which may be why its proponents feel compelled to constantly hammer you in the head with it until you finally relent merely because your head hurts.

More importantly, it's a blatant act of moving the goalposts. It's an attempt to redefine the term "racism" in a way that effectively silences whites and cripples their ability to address the topic with any level of meaning, honesty, or emotion.

You may counter that I'm merely whining at the fact that my privileges are being taken away from me, but what non-masochistic human being isn't going to get upset about having things taken from them? You can take candy from either a baby or a 90-year-old, and they'll both still cry.

When attempting to define terms, I suppose that dictionaries can in some minor ways be helpful. Webster's defines "racism" thusly:

1
: *a belief that race is the primary determinant of human traits and capacities and that racial differences produce an inherent superiority of a particular race*
2
: *racial prejudice or discrimination*

OK, I've looked over that definition many times and still haven't seen an addendum that says, "....but only when white people are doing it." So for the time being, the official definition of "racism" does not contain any such "whites only" clause.

But according to Luke Visconti, a white man who is the CEO of something called DiversityInc, such dictionary definitions of racism are indeed "too white." From a cursory glance of his website, I suspect that everything may be "too white" for Visconti—possibly even himself. If he were offered the magical ability to molt his skin like a snake and emerge as a coal-black Haitian, I tend to believe he'd accept the offer, provided there was no salary cut.

All of his memes are familiar and threadbare, and he barfs them up like a baby bird regurgitating a half-digested worm to please its mother. Like many of his ilk, Visconti attempts to split semantic pubes—he distinguishes "racism" from "bigotry" and "prejudice." He says that while one may run across the occasional black bigot, such lone wolves do not have the institutional power to discriminate against whites in the way that our government and media routinely discriminate against blacks by...um...actually, he didn't provide any examples of how the government and media currently do this.

As much as I'd hate to crawl into the minds of others, I'd say that nearly everyone on this filthy little planet holds their own hatreds and stereotypes and prejudices and postjudices. And you know what? So long as I'm not getting hurt, I'm cool with that. Bartender—serve up a round of hatred for everyone!

Still, saying that "only whites can be racist" is blood libel against all whites, and as a white guy who doesn't really give a hoot either way about being white unless you want to stigmatize or extort or harm me because of it, I'm going to toot my referee whistle, throw my penalty flag on the ground, and say you're being unfair.

They'll talk all the livelong day about how whites accrued tremendous power, but they'll run away like frightened church mice from pondering *how* whites were able to achieve this in the first place and why other groups were unable to beat them to it. Obviously, technological and organizational prowess during the right historical moments were not factors—they've already ruled out those explanations. Nor have any other groups besides whites *ever* practiced slavery or ethnic favoritism or territorial aggression. No, it's all explained by hatred and evil and unfairness and racism and other silly demon words designed to scare four-year-old girls in a horror movie where all the ghosts are white.

All of this pain and all of these headaches could have been averted if the authors of *Is Everyone Really Equal?* had actually considered their question, paused for a moment, and answered "No."

Try it—it only hurts the first couple times you admit it to yourself. The observable and demonstrable fact that *everyone isn't really equal* explains so many cultural phenomena that the social justice warriors limply attempt to explain with their insane, convoluted illogic. It's silly to claim that only whites may be racist. But you may have a point if you said that only whites do it so *well*.

19

Since When Are Egyptians Not White?

I don't care what color the ancient Egyptians were, but then again, I'm not an Afrocentrist. But if one day in the distant future after a series of debilitating strokes I were to become an Afrocentrist, it would be necessary for me to picture the ancient Egyptians as black. I'll explain why in a minute.

Irascible octogenarian multibillionaire media oligarch Rupert Murdoch says that Egyptians are white. He also says you need to calm down if you disagree. Twentieth Century Fox—one of Murdoch's many long, slithering, pipe-snaking media tentacles—will soon be releasing the biblical epic *Exodus: Gods and Kings*, and already the howling uteri of the social-justice battalions are squalling that the film is by its very nature racist since Caucasian actors portray the main Egyptian characters.

According to the film's director Ridley Scott, the Caucasoid cast was neither a stab at racial revisionism nor an attempt at historical accuracy; it was a matter of financial expediency. Scott told *Variety*:

> *I can't mount a film of this budget, where I have to rely on tax rebates in Spain, and say that my lead actor is Mohammad so-and-so from such-and-such. I'm just not going to get it financed.*

Still, this didn't stop the complaints. Nothing ever stops the complaints.

Responding to the complaints, Murdoch caused a minor Twitstorm with a series of three tweets:

> *Moses film attacked on Twitter for all white cast. Since when are Egyptians not white? All I know are.*
> 8:07PM 28 Nov 2014

> *Everybody-attacks last tweet. Of course Egyptians are Middle Eastern, but far from black. They treated blacks as slaves.*
> 8:22PM 28 Nov 2014

> *Okay, there are many shades of color. Nothing racist about that, so calm down!*
> 8:53PM 28 Nov 2014

Apparently it's an emotionally charged topic for a lot of people. Since Egypt was one of the greatest ancient civilizations, it's understandable that competing modern ethnic groups would try to call dibs on it.

Wikipedia has a whole page devoted to the "Ancient Egyptian race controversy," and if you squint hard enough to read between all the disclaimers about how race isn't real and that all respectable modern anthropologists will tell you it doesn't even exist, it covers the spectrum of popular hypotheses and theories about the genetic makeup of ancient Egypt's movers and shakers. These range from the Black Egyptian hypothesis (they were full-blooded black Africans); to the Asiatic Race Theory (they were descended from Middle Easterners); to the Caucasian/Hamitic hypothesis (they were white Euros); to the Turanid race hypothesis (they were Mongols); to the Dynastic race theory (they were an elite set of Mesopotamian conquerors).

Wikipedia's "Population history of Egypt" page gets a smidge more specific with the science. Modern Egyptians, at least, possess a "non-recombining portion of the Y chromosome...[that is] much more similar to those of the Middle East than to any sub-Saharan African population." It also avers that "blood typing of dynastic mummies found ABO frequencies to be most similar to modern Egyptians." It adds that one famous DNA study concluded that "Ancient Egyptians were indeed most similar to people from Western Asia"—Western Asia being a fashionable new geographic term for what used to be called the Middle East.

If that's the case, then Ol' Rupert was half-right—while probably not "white" in the Nordic sense, King Tut and his ilk definitely weren't "black" in the Ferguson-rioter sense, either. The ancient Egyptians were most likely somewhat Middle Eastern in appearance, and I can live with that. I don't have a sphinx in that fight—nor an Anubis, for that matter.

The main group that appears to have an emotional problem with the idea that ancient Egypt was not ruled by coal-colored, woolly-haired men of distinctly Negroidal features would be Afrocentric scholars. Sure, the earnest Asian or European ethnocentrist might like to claim Egypt as a notch in their ancestral belt, but they don't absolutely *depend* on it like the Afrocentrist must.

So why is ancient Egypt the Crown Jewels, the Hope Diamond, the Holy Grail, Excalibur, and the NASCAR Sprint Cup all rolled into one for the Afrocentrist?

Stepping on this topic as gingerly as I can manage emotionally, let's take a deep breath and look at it from a different angle: What has the area that is now known as Swaziland really ever given the world in terms of culture and technology? How about Gabon? Dare I suggest the Central African Republic? No? What about Angola? Hmm? Still drawing blanks?

Ancient Egypt was undeniably African. But was it "black" in the commonly understood modern sense? Probably not. And if you remove ancient Egypt from the "black" column, some cruel-hearted types might suggest that you're left looking at an appalling dearth not only of technical innovations, but even of recorded history, originating from the wild southern lands that are kept safely away from Egypt by the massive and deadly Sahara Desert. If they can't claim Egypt, they can't claim much.

I could be wrong. But it'd be nice to see some proof. Typically when I ask people to show me any compelling evidence of high civilization and technological achievement that developed south of the Sahara, they usually point me back to Egypt. And that sucks—at least if you're black, it does.

20

Santa Claus: Still White

Although Santa Claus doesn't exist, I am neverthe-less convinced that he is white. I take it as a mat-ter of faith that he is as white as his beard and as white as the polar ice caps. As a pale male of exclu-sively Northern European descent, I also choose to believe that Santa Claus is a man—a *heterosexual* man who enjoys giving Mrs. Claus a right good rogering from time to time.

Aisha Harris would disagree. Aisha is a blogger for slate.com. She shares a first name with the girl who was married to Muhammad at age six and consum-mated their marriage at the unripened age of nine—while Ol' Mo was 53—but I didn't see this fact mentioned in the article that set off a diarrheal blast of news coverage.

The essay was called "Santa Claus Should Not Be a White Man Anymore," and forgive me if I think it's a wee bit uppity for Aisha to presume she has the authority to make such declarations. Aisha writes of the shame and pain and confusion and heartache she'd experience every holiday season when she walked out into the Scary Big White World and was ruthlessly confronted with "pale" Santas who had "skin as pink as bubble gum." Aisha failed to note that if she were still living in her ancestral homeland, she likely wouldn't be concerned with such trifles. Back in those non-wintry climes, she might even know what horseflies taste like.

The language Aisha uses in her article to deride Santa's commonly understood physiognomy would likely raise the hackles of microaggression-sniffing progressive watchdogs were they applied to anyone else besides white men. Harris called Santa "melanin-deficient," a "fat old white man," an "old white male," and a "fat white guy":

> ...I propose that America abandon Santa-as-fat-old-white-man and create a new symbol of Christmas cheer. From here on out, Santa Claus should be a penguin....That's right: a penguin....Why, you ask? For one thing, making Santa Claus an animal rather than an old white male could spare millions of nonwhite kids the insecurity and shame that I remember from childhood.

A young black-and-white penguin, you say? Preferably one that would likely morph into a young hermaphroditic rainbow-colored penguin? And then a young human in a hermaphroditic rainbow-colored penguin costume because the animal-rights activists complained? I don't like where this is headed at *all*, Aisha. Not one tiny little bit. You get a lump of coal from me this Christmas.

Still, I find it incumbent upon myself to apologize for some of my brethren who joked that if Santa Claus was black, he'd be breaking into houses with an empty bag and leaving with it full. That so-called "joke" was not funny, nor was it appropriate in these very, very, *very* sensitive times of change and progress.

On the Fox News channel, blonde politico-vixen Megyn Kelly made sport of Aisha's let's-turn-Santa-into-a-penguin screed:

> *For all you kids watching at home, Santa just is white....Santa is what he is....Just because it makes you feel uncomfortable doesn't mean it has to change, you know? I mean, Jesus was a white man, too....He was a historical figure, I mean, that's a verifiable fact, as is Santa—I just want the kids watching to know that.*

In the face of the monster media shit-storm that her comments set off, Kelly would later claim that she was only joking when she said that Santa exists and is white. I've scrutinized the video over and over as if it was the Zapruder film and I still can't tell whether she was serious or not. I'm not even sure it matters.

Naturally, it wasn't Aisha Harris's inane and childish plea for a biracial Santa Penguin that led to torrents of media mockery; it was Megyn Kelly's comments that both Jesus and Santa Claus are white.

It was widely insisted that Jesus was not white, he was Jewish. This would lead to the conclusion that Jews are not white. No further questions, Your Honor.

Most of the snark bombs were directed at Kelly's allegation that Santa Claus is white. CNN's Don Lemon, whose skin is more the color of a coconut husk than a lemon, gleefully declared that "Santa Claus is black," and yet no one complained. From behind his desk in Manhattan, Jon Stewart (*né* Leibowitz) mocked the rural rubes who believe in a white Santa: "Yes, West Virginia, there is a Santa Claus." MSNBC's Chris Hayes, who is exactly like Rachel Maddow but with far less testosterone, scoffed at the "Fear of a Black Santa."

They reminded us that Santa Claus is based on St. Nicholas, a Greek who lived in what is now Turkey and would probably have had olive-colored skin, no freckles, and thus not be a white man at all.

It's true that linguistic corruption eventually transformed "Saint Nikolaos" into "Santa Claus." It's also true that the real-life St. Nick was known for his gift-giving ways. But that's where most of the similarities seem to end. Otherwise, the St. Nicholas legend veers off into other weird pathways such as how he liked to help sailors and how he saved three poor daughters from becoming hookers and the time where he resurrected three boys who'd been chopped to death by a butcher.

Other major elements of the Santa Claus legend seem to have been supplied by Northern European mythology that got subsumed into Christianity as it conquered the continent. Northern Germans and Scandinavians celebrated a holiday called Yule around the winter solstice. During Yule season, the white-bearded pagan god Odin would traverse the skies by night on his eight-legged horse. Children would place boots near the chimney filled with straw for Odin's horse to eat. In the morning they'd awake to find the straw replaced with gifts and candy. It is thought that Odin's eight-legged horse would later morph into eight tiny reindeer and the boots would become Christmas stockings.

The British, Dutch, and others would add several layers to the Santa myth, but what's important is that beyond St. Nicholas's Greek origins, everything else about the legend appears to have germinated and developed in Northern Europe. (Further modifications were made to the Santa Claus myth in America, but Thomas Nast and Clement Clarke Moore also had skin as pink as bubble gum.) Santa Claus is a primarily Northern European cultural icon and therefore about as white as it gets.

Yet here come the justice-obsessed hordes from warmer climes, seeking to diddle with the European collective unconscious yet again. In other contexts what they're doing would be called "cultural appropriation," "colonialism," or even "intolerance." Amid the Aisha Harris/Megyn Kelly hubbub, a white teacher in New Mexico was "disciplined" for telling a black student that Santa Claus is white.

First they tell us they don't want Black Pete to be black, and now they're telling us that they don't want Santa to be white. I think it's time to tell them to stop telling us what to do.

If you don't like that, well, go and invent your *own* holiday fantasy figures. Better yet, track down your biological father and have *him* get you some toys for Christmas. We gave you the presidency, but I'm *not* going to let you have Santa Claus. Every man has his limits, and this one is mine. I'm drawing a line in the snow, and if you cross it, you're risking the wrath of Odin.

21

A World Without Western Civ

At 2016's Republican National Convention in Cleveland, none of the speakers used the phrase "white people." Anti-racists, however, need to make EVERYTHING about race, so they made it about white people anyway.

Appearing on a panel helmed by MSNBC's lesbian-faced Chris Hayes, an old white man named Charles Pierce of *Esquire* magazine racially taunted fellow old white man Steve King, a Republican congressman from Iowa:

> *If you're really optimistic, you can say that this is the last time that old white people will command the Republican Party's attention, its platform, its public face. That hall is wired by loud, unhappy, dissatisfied white people.*

King tossed the bomb back in Pierce's lap:

This "old white people" business does get a little tired, Charlie. I'd ask you to go back through history and figure out, where are these contributions that have been made by these other categories of people that you're talking about, where did any other subgroup of people contribute more to civilization?

A fat black female panelist began hootin' and hollerin' and acting as if she caught the vapors, whereupon Hayes scolded King that white people were responsible for Hitler and Stalin.

MSNBC would later describe King's comments as "jaw-dropping." The *Washington Post* called his comments "weird." The website Quartz referred to his utterly rational and dispassionate question as "an awkward, racist rant." And *Esquire* deemed his question to be "batshit" crazy.

I suppose that when you don't want to answer a question, it's best to gaslight the person who asked it. Asked later about his now-infamous question, a remorse-free King noted that none of the apopleptic co-panelists had bothered to answer it:

You go back and Google "old white people," "old white men," [and] you'll find that that comes out of the mouth of leftists constantly. They have decided it's open season on white people in America from an ideological standpoint. And I hope it stops there, but somebody needs to stand up for the contributions that have been made by Western Civilization. And if we disparage our roots, if we disparage what makes this a great nation, then we'll lose the formula for being an even greater nation. So I stood up for our foundation, for our history, for our culture, of Western Civilization, and I said so. And if you'll notice, Chris Hayes didn't want to go down that path after that.

Of course, this didn't stop others from attempting to go down that path. The oniony-looking Rebecca Onion of Slate asserted that it made "no sense" to judge groups by their historical inventions, despite the fact that a given racial group's level of technological innovation is tightly correlated with its relative success and prosperity. Writing for Salon, a certain Sarah Watts didn't appear to be joking when she credited Africans for inventing "humanity." (I suppose other inventions were hard to come by.) She also typed with a straight face that non-American and non-European "subgroups" like Asia, Latin America, Africa, and the Middle East are "almost solely responsible for what we consider modern society."

There are reams of evidence of technological innovations by the ancient Chinese, the ancient Indians, and the ancient Semites—emphasis on the "ancient."

For example, the Chinese invented gunpowder. But for some reason these perennial warriors and kung-fu fighters weren't savvy enough to use their invention as a weapon of war.

The ancient Indians are widely credited with inventing the numerical system we currently use. But they certainly didn't invent calculus like Newton and Leibniz did.

Most uncomfortable for egalitarians and their ilk is that there are vast landmasses—sometimes entire continents—where the indigenous inhabitants have invented virtually nothing. Sub-Saharan Africans are not known for contributing much to rocket science, and black Americans are so underrepresented as inventors that everyone has heard a gorillion times about the mulatto who improved blood-storage methods and George Washington Carver's wondrous dalliances with the magical peanut. The so-called "Native Americans" are credited with inventing the spinning top, which somehow proved incapable of defending them against the white man and his guns. And Australia's aborigines? Well, let's not talk about them, because they'd be embarrassed. Peruvians can take pride in developing the art of potato cultivation. And I've already covered the Mexicans and their nachos.

If you were to note every manmade item within your field of vision, chances are that nearly every last gadget and trinket was invented by a white man. According to Charles Murray's book *Human Accomplishment*, whites have historically dominated the fields of physics, math, chemistry, medicine, biology, and technology.

What's grossly ironic is the specter of people using white computers hooked up to white electricity sent across white power grids to criticize the very white people who made their whining possible. Even worse is the ubiquity of white people pejoratively using the term "white people" as if it somehow doesn't apply to them. That right there is a collective mental illness for the ages.

White technology has doubled lifespans across the globe and yanked several human subgroups out of the Stone Age. This makes certain white people feel guilty. It also apparently makes lots of nonwhite people resentful.

Those who wish to downplay or outright deny the vastness of white contributions to the world's technological and civilizational development claim that to even dare giving credit where it's due will immediately lead to millions of slaughtered nonwhites. That's an insane leap of logic, but they keep on a-leapin'.

When all else fails, press the Holocaust Button. As noted, Chris Hayes mentioned Hitler rather than answer Steve King's question. Many others who dodged King's question immediately brought up the Holocaust and slavery and colonialism as Western Civilization's true "inventions." The *Washington Post* quoted an Indian female historian who felt the need to bring up concentration camps, atomic bombs, the Crusades, slavery, and witch hunts as distinctly white contributions to the world.

Apparently it's a virtue to be so dumb that you decapitate people like the Aztecs or eat them like the African cannibals rather than being brainy enough to develop an atomic bomb.

Slate's Rebecca Onion warns that "the idea of white technological superiority has often served as justification for oppressing or displacing nonwhite people." But flip that around—denying white technological contributions and distilling all of white history into one massive blood libel of torture and enslavement of nonwhites can serve as justification for displacing white people. Remember, this whole controversy started when an old white male progressive could barely contain his righteously masochistic glee at the idea of "old white people" dying out. Much—if not most, or even all—of political guilt-tripping is rooted in psychological projection.

22

Fear of an Erudite White

Jared Taylor. *White Identity: Racial Consciousness in the 21st Century.* New Century Books, 2011. 342 pp.

It's hard to find things to hate about Jared Taylor, and that's what his enemies seem to hate about him the most.

In a culture where "the racist"—who is *always* white—has been the most crudely stereotyped stock villain over the past generation, Taylor stubbornly (yet politely) breaks the mold. You can tell he's a different breed merely by the way he pronounces the word "white"—rather than an illiterate cracker drawl that sounds like "waht," he ever-so-properly aspirates the "wh" so that it sounds instead like "hwite."

He's one erudite white. And they hate that. The foot soldiers of egalitarian thought control would rather that all "racists" range from mildly to severely retarded. But to their preciously inviolable little narrative's detriment, Taylor is a trilingual Yale grad who has written two books, edited several anthologies, and published the monthly newsletter *American Renaissance* for two decades. What confounds, perplexes, and infuriates his antagonists is that he's obviously not stupid, yet he stubbornly refuses to see the world as they do.

Bereft of solid arguments against him, they rely on the crutch of false accusations. He's been consistently mislabeled a "white supremacist," an odd moniker for someone who once said, "I think Asians are objectively superior to whites by just about any measure that you can come up with in terms of what are the ingredients for a successful society."

He gets hammered for being a "fascist," although he insists he favors unhindered freedom of association, which is a less coercive system than what exists even in modern America, not to mention Nazi Germany (although everyone always has to mention Nazi Germany in these sort of discussions, anyway).

And though he's always painted as a "hatemonger," I've never seen him huff and puff with genocidal glee at a specific racial demographic's literal death as that fat little hamster Tim Wise has. In fact, I've only witnessed hatred being directed *at* Jared Taylor. At a scheduled 2007 debate in Halifax, a crew of violent agitators wearing masks—you know, just like the Klan!—forcibly ejected Taylor from the room before the debate started. Anti-racist busybodies were able to shut down two American Renaissance conferences in a row merely by engaging in such compassionately humanitarian tactics as phoning in death threats to the hotels where they were to be held. They even show up to hassle him when he holds press conferences about being hassled.

This is not the behavior of intellectuals, but of religious fanatics. Their hysterically censorious actions are not those of people who feel they've won the debate, but of those who fear that if their god were held up to the harsh light of logical scrutiny, it might shrivel up and die.

White Identity is Jared Taylor's first full-length solo opus since 1992's *Paved With Good Intentions* and is written in the same dispassionately lean, brick-by-brick, Wall of Facts style. He presents his case like a District Attorney, minus the moralistic grandstanding and cheap appeals to emotion.

Taylor notes that by today's definition of what it has supposedly always meant to be an American, every US president up to JFK would be deemed a virulently hateful white supremacist merely for expressing the sort of group instincts that remain uncontested—even loudly encouraged—among nonwhites to this day. He says American society's downward slide was greatly enabled by the 1944 publication of Gunnar Myrdal's landmark socio-logical tome *An American Dilemma*, which posited that white racism was the primary (if not sole) cause of black poverty. Nearly ten years later came Gor-don Allport's *The Nature of Prejudice*, which pro-posed the idea of "contact theory"—that racial and ethnic tension were caused by a *lack* of contact among divergent racial groups rather than, say, unwanted, coerced, and persistent contact in cramped quarters while competing for dwindling resources. Armed with the untested and unproved hypotheses that white racism was alone to blame for black underachievement and that lack of con-tact rather than direct contact led to racial tension, social theorists and their political bedfellows set about to radically transform American demograph-ics.

In one passage Taylor trots out an Orwellian litany of American politicians mouthing nigglingly slight variations on the platitude that "Diversity is our greatest strength," yet his open challenge for any-one to explain what benefits diversity has brought us beyond a wider selection of restaurants remains unanswered. He presents a devastating case that forced integration has been a titanic failure as well as a direct cause of cultural Balkanization and national decline. In neighborhoods, churches, prisons, and school cafeterias—everywhere that they aren't forced by law to mingle—the seemingly intractable natural tendency is for ethnic groups to self-segregate.

Taylor cites the work of Finnish researcher Tatu Vanhanen, who posits that ethnically homogenous societies are far less conflict-prone than "diverse" ones, as well as Harvard political scientist Robert Putnam, who, against his better wishes, concluded after massive research that individuals in "diverse" societies tend to be less happy, trusting, and far more alienated than those in societies founded on ethnic kinship.

Taylor spends several pages documenting a growing, and almost entirely unreported, violent race war between blacks and Mexicans in California mainly because it resoundingly subverts the fiction that ethnic tension would cease to exist if white racism—or even white people—were removed from the equation.

Taylor argues that the stubborn persistence of ethnocentrism and a tendency to favor those who look like us are the result of deep-rooted natural tribal instincts rather than artificial racist indoctrination. He cites studies where infants favor photos of people who most resemble themselves and where adults, despite decades of exposure to anti-racist propaganda and their own deeply cherished egalitarian beliefs, tend to do the same thing. Blood is apparently not only thicker than water; it's thicker than everything.

As if the unprecedented social experiment of pouring several dissimilar schools of fish into the same aquarium and pretending they won't fight over food and territory wasn't foolhardy enough, Taylor sees special danger in the severely unequal application of cultural taboos regarding racial pride:

> White racism is commonly alleged to be the great obstacle to harmonious race relations in the United States, but whites are the only group that actually subscribes to the goal of eliminating race consciousness and that actively polices its members for signs of such consciousness....The only occasion on which it is acceptable for whites to speak collectively as whites is to apologize....Some whites have gone well beyond color-blindness and see their race as uniquely guilty and without moral standing....At what point would it be legitimate for whites to act in their own group interests? When they become a minority? When they are no more than 30 percent of the population? Ten percent?...Eventually, whites will come to understand that to dismantle and even demonize white racial conscious-

ness while other races cultivate racial consciousness is a
fatal form of unilateral disarmament.

As with his earlier *Paved With Good Intentions*, Taylor relentlessly documents sickening heaps of hateful and genocidal anti-white rhetoric that in many cases not only goes unpunished but is instead rewarded by politicians. After openly encouraging the rape of white women and the wholesale slitting of white throats, Amiri Baraka was appointed New Jersey's poet laureate. In the same year that Chicano activist Mario Obledo boasted that California was becoming a Hispanic state and that "anyone who don't like it...should go back to Europe," President Bill Clinton awarded him the Medal of Freedom.

The mainstream media is likewise criminally complicit in maintaining such dangerously unsustainable double standards, perhaps most profoundly when it comes to interracial violence. If white youth anywhere in America were doing anything along the lines of "polar bear hunting," you'd never hear the end of it. But as it stands, you've probably never heard of polar bear hunting.

Such howling double standards breed like viruses when dealing with ideology-driven social engineers who somehow see no logical errors in insisting that "race" doesn't exist but that "racism" exists anywhere that white people aren't constantly apologizing.

For the time being, the majority of American whites have been terrified into silence by a single word that is wielded like a Taser against any Caucasian American who refuses to submit to the program. The word "racist" is used exclusively against whites to immobilize any stirrings of group consciousness. It is swung like a hammer at the skull of any white person who still has the nerve to say they aren't profoundly ashamed of their own skin.

But if current trends continue and whites slip into despised-minority status as they most certainly will, the game will change. When one's life choices winnow down between being murdered by an angry dark mob and being called a racist, the word "racist" won't seem so bad at all. A tipping point will come where group consciousness will seem far less loathsome than group extinction.

The recent rash of hysterical "anti-fascist" reactions against Jared Taylor are emotional rather than logical. So rather than debate him—I've yet to see anyone try to engage him in rational discourse whom he didn't wind up decimating—the order of the day is to dub him a "racist," silence him, and declare victory.

Good luck with all that while it lasts. Ironically, such cowardly rhetorical tactics and triumphalist ethnic taunting will awaken a sleeping giant. Sooner rather than later, the egalitarian left's unapologetic bullies will be forced to deal with the big white monster they've helped create.

23

The Browning

A paper released in March 2010 predicted that year might be the one in which nonwhite births outnumber white births for the first time in US history.

"White" is, of course, a relative term, and the study in question doesn't include Hispanics under its Big White Tent. In fact, it's the highly race-conscious Spics who are squeezing out fetuses much more rapidly than the crackers, 'groids, slopes, and everyone else.

Do not fear me or what I am about to say. I am here to strengthen the ties that bind. It is my sincere belief that of all people on this planet, I am the only man alive who can bring everyone together. I mingled with and attempted miscegenation with nonwhites long before it became fashionable and eons before it became compulsory. I have taken great pains and spent several years doing field research to establish that poor black people understand me better than affluent white people do, so I approach this topic with a rare degree of compassion and insight.

This morning I left my pearly-white wife and blue-eyed son at home in our 86%-black 'hood as I headed to work. I listened to the Jew Neil Diamond on the radio and stopped for some Southern "country cooking" grilled up and served for $2.99 by a Chinese woman and her slant-eyed husband. At work, I mix in smoothly with Colombians and Ecuadorians and Guyanese and Cameroonians and Ethiopians and Jews and even black Americans who call each other "brother" without fear of being deemed racist.

So it's not as if I have a problem getting along with "people of color." For the most part, I get along better with them and respect them more than I do modern white Americans.

I realize that many of you are ecstatic to the point of auto-orgasm at the fact that whites are becoming an American minority. You exult in some sick, primitive, religious notion of karmic retribution and chickens coming home to roost. You believe—or more properly, you have been persuaded—that white supremacy is mankind's primary enemy and that this rumbling you hear as America's demographic tectonic plates shift is actually the loudly joyous sound of a New Era of racial harmony and all-around slap-happy get-togetherness. Without much more than a wing and a prayer, you are convinced that nonwhites are not prone to, nor even morally capable of, ethnic violence or tendencies toward unfairly favoring their own "kind." You think a sudden interracial orgy will erupt, permanently breeding out all discernible ethnic differences and creating an oatmeal-colored Unitribe who feels as if they've "been there, done that" regarding ethnic tension and that the very topic of race is SOOOOOOOOOO 1965.

Good luck with all that.

I'm not so hopeful. I believe the current conditions point more toward catastrophe than harmony.

Here's why:

THE DOUBLE STANDARD

White Americans are forbidden from expressing ethnic pride—or, at the least, there's a grudging tolerance of specific national pride such as being Irish, but NEVER just being "white"—while all nonwhites are free to bask proudly in their genetic juices, general or specific, without fear of being labeled bigots. Social double standards are dangerous and never lead to unity. Either everyone should be discouraged from expressing ethnic pride, or everyone should be allowed to express it, no matter how moronic or distasteful it may appear to others. I'm in favor of the latter. But for the time being, it looks as if whites are the only ones who got the memo that we're supposed to be going "post-racial."

THERE'S NO PROOF THAT THIS NOBLE "EXPERIMENT" HAS EVER WORKED

Multiculturalism demands we celebrate the fact that the only thing we have in common is that we have nothing in common. This post-racial utopia we've been promised has been warmly embraced as irrefutable social science, although I haven't seen a sliver of evidence to support the idea that this will work or has ever worked in the past. I haven't been shown any solid examples of poly-ethnic, poly-lingual, poly-religious nations that have been, as the environmentalists like to say, "sustainable" for long periods. The historical record tends to show that these are preconditions for a nation falling apart rather than staying together and that unity tends to be a much stronger adhesive force than diversity. In fact, the most comprehensive study I've yet to see on the subject revealed that ethnic diversity makes people less happy and weakens communities rather than strengthening them.

IMMIGRATION HYPOCRISY

I don't see anyone saying that Venezuela needs more Swedes or that China needs more Belgians, but I hear a lot of people screaming that Western countries need to spread their legs open to non-Westerners. Yes, you can say we're a "nation of immigrants" from one side of your mouth, but the other side's bitching that those immigrants have been far too white for far too long. There's even some speculation that white Europeans may have occupied North America ten millennia before Columbus ever stubbed his toe on it. But if, in fact, white immigrants only arrived here after Columbus and it was wrong for them to overwhelm the cultures that occupied this land, why is it suddenly a good thing that another process of genetic displacement and culture-dispossession is occurring? Two wrongs don't make a right, at least not according to the rules of logic. And for all the bitching everyone does about the evils of white majorities, 21 of the top 22 nations on the UN's "Quality of Life" scale are majority-white, so they must be doing something right. Why, then, is it considered insane to challenge the party dogma that making these nations less white will lead to improved living conditions? Why is it deemed a thought crime even to ask?

Throw away the peace signs and rainbow flags and take a serious look at evolutionary social psychology and the competition for resources. I believe people are hard-wired to be tribal, which is why the government spends so much time and pays so many ideological-marketing experts trying to rewire you.

I believe that whatever used to be our "common fabric" is now in tatters. I anticipate that in America, every color in the rainbow is headed for some mighty rough times. And more than anything, I hope I'm wrong.

Like I said, I know how to get along when I want to, but I'm not so sure about everyone else. I don't plan on antagonizing anyone because they're different from me, but neither will I lie down like an obedient white lamb in case I get antagonized.

And I'll teach my little white son never to hate anyone because they're different from him, but I'll kick in the fucking skull of anyone who attacks him because he's white.

Sounds fair to me. Do we have a deal?

24

1 + 1 = You're a Racist

Piper Harron is an unhappy-looking black woman whose mood would be greatly improved if white male math professors would just 'fess up to their unearned privilege and quit their jobs. She is currently a "temporary assistant professor" in mathematics at the University of Hawaii at Manoa, and I think we can all agree that this is the first time any of us has ever heard of that school.

Piper holds a Ph.D. in Mathematics from Princeton University, which sounds impressive until you take into account the mathematical fact that a study from Princeton reveals that blacks are given a handicap of 230 SAT points compared to whites when it comes to admissions standards.

On her resume, she makes the startling and mathematically improbable claim that during her eleven years of collegiate studies, she not only "survived external and internalized misogyny," she also suffered the horrors of "external and internalized racism." What are the odds?

In a recent blog post titled "Get Out of the Way," she implies that white males are impeding her from getting a better job than, you know, a gig as a "temporary assistant professor" position at some no-name school in Honolulu:

> *If you are a white cis man (meaning you identify as male and you were assigned male at birth) you almost certainly should resign from your position of power. That's right, please quit....What can universities do? Well, that's easier. Stop hiring white cis men (except as needed to get/retain people who are not white cis men) until the problem goes away....I know you're not going to quit your job, but I want you to understand that you should....Not to alarm you, but statistically speaking you are the problem. Your very presence. I can't tell you what is the best strategy for you to stop blocking my path. I can just ask that you please get out of my way.*

Ms. Harron is not the only person of non-maleness who thinks that math is a thinly disguised weapon to impose white male supremacy upon unfairly marginalized groups. Harvard-trained mathematician Cathy O'Neil—whose homeliness cannot be measured in mere integers—wrote a book called *Weapons of Math Destruction* which argued that "Big

Data" has conspired to use algorithms for the sinister purpose of squashing everyone who isn't a white male under a huge white-male thumb.

Math teachers at middle schools across this once-fine nation can treat themselves to a six-week online course called "Teaching Social Justice through Secondary Mathematics," which asserts—with zero mathematical documentation, mind you—that "For centuries, mathematics has been used as a dehumanizing tool":

> *Do you ask students to think deeply about global and local social justice issues within your mathematics classroom? This education and teacher training course will help you blend secondary math instruction with topics such as inequity, poverty, and privilege to transform students into global thinkers and mathematicians.*

One wonders whether they want social-justice teachers to ask their students to think deeply about mathematics.

A recent paper—alleged to be scholarly—titled "A Framework for Understanding Whiteness in Mathematics Education" states, without one shred of statistical data to bolster their allegations, that:

> *Naming white institutional spaces, as well as identifying the mechanisms that oppress and privilege students, can give those who work in the field of mathematics education*

specific ideas of how to better combat racist structures....A lot of times in whiteness literature, we talk about the refusal to pathologize whiteness, and this is a case....For African Americans, for Native Americans, for Latinos in mathematics, we attribute something internally to the child or internally to the culture that's making them achieve lower.

Short version: Blacks and Latinos score much lower than whites on math tests because they've internalized the false stereotype that they score lower than whites on math tests, a racist fiction that couldn't possibly have originated from the quantifiable fact that blacks and Latinos scored lower than whites on math tests in the first place.

I remember hearing the ludicrous, stillborn idea that "math is racist" all the way back in the early 1990s. A 1990 paper called "Western Mathematics: the secret weapon of cultural imperialism" claims that "western mathematics" was "one of the most powerful weapons in the imposition of western culture." It then goes on to argue that "western mathematics" originated in India, China, and the Middle East, which means they aren't really Western, anyway, so why are they even bitching?

When it comes to pupils who score higher than 750 on the math portion of the SATs, Asians outnumber whites nearly 2-1 in raw numbers, despite that fact that whites outnumber Asians by a clip of about 10-1 in the USA.

In the only way we know how to quantify such things—by scores on math tests, duh!—it would appear that if math is indeed "racist," it is biased strongly against non-Asians.

According to test scores, math absolutely hates black people. On average, they score a measly 428 in math on the SATs, a robust 170 points behind Asians. Clumsy attempts to improve black math scores have led to what is known as "The L.A. Math Proficiency Test," which has gone through several humorous incarnations over the years. In Manitoba, a teacher was disciplined for asking their students to calculate "how many 'tricks' per day three prostitutes must turn to support their pimp Rufus's cocaine habit." In 2016, a retiring Alabama teacher was put on leave after allegedly posing this question to her math class:

> Tyrone knocked up 4 girls in the gang. There are 20 girls in his gang. What is the exact percentage of girls Tyrone knocked up?

SAT scores in math are also virulently misogynist, seeing as women average 32 fewer points than men on them, a pattern which has remained unbroken since the 1970s.

Trying to inject unquantifiable social-justice pieties into a discipline which operates with cold and brutal efficiency is a severe case of overstepping the boundaries. At the very most, dumb and purely emotional ideas such as "social justice" should be confined to the philosophy and religious departments.

Like science, math is amoral and non-ideological. Those who can't differentiate between math and social justice are, as my father used to say, people who can't tell their asses from a hole in the ground.

25

The Spooks of Hazzard

Only in America can white people organize an event intended to mock poor Southern whites, have black people crying that it's racist against blacks, and then have white people apologizing to blacks about it.

That's what happened in the small Arizona town of Queen Creek, whose black population is a hearty and robust one third of one percent. Back in May 2013, as part of Queen Creek High School's "Spirit Week," the school sponsored "Redneck Day," which principal Tom Lindsey claims was intended not to honor, but to satirize, po'-white Southern culture as exemplified in the frighteningly popular A&E reality show *Duck Dynasty*.

Duck Dynasty is part of a recent wave of TV shows that depict what used to be known as normal Americans as exotic and endangered creatures on a wild-game preserve, almost always for comic effect to amuse presumably sophisticated and non-prejudiced urbanites and coastal dwellers. Other shows in this genre include *Here Comes Honey Boo Boo, Swamp People, Buckwild*, and *Redneck Island*.

Not only aren't such stereotypes discouraged—Hollywood's masters of reality eagerly applaud and lavishly finance sweepingly negative cultural oversimplifications that in any other ethnic context would be labeled as hate speech.

On "Redneck Day" in Queen Creek, one student—apparently a Southern transplant—draped himself in a Rebel flag, which nitpickers will remind you is often incorrectly referred to as a "Confederate flag." He was asked to remove it, which he promptly did.

And then came the backlash. Local black race hustlers were the first to pile on. The Southern Poverty Law Center, which should at least be honest and change its name to The Anti-Southern Rich People's Law Center, stuck its hate-sniffing beak into the situation. And now the Department of Justice is investigating the school for possible civil-rights violations.

"We apologize to any people who, because of the word (redneck), were offended," groveled the school principal. Mind you, he wasn't apologizing to American whites of meager means—the untold millions whose forefathers came as indentured servants, whose ancestors died in the hundreds of thousands in the Civil War, and who have historically been pitted in economic and cultural competition against blacks ever since the original indentured servants were driven off the plantations and into the backwoods and hills—he was apologizing to *black people*.

Didn't matter. The perpetually offended were out for a lynching, and they smelled blood.

Perhaps smelling money as well, civil-rights attorney Steve Montoya of Phoenix said, "The Confederacy represents the horrible institution of slavery, and that is a direct attack on African-Americans."

"I'm sitting here crying and praying," wailed Ozetta Kirby, vice president of a local NAACP chapter, whose grandson Marcus is a student at Queen Creek. "This thing really got to Marcus," Kirby said. "No kid should have to go through that. We all know the connotation of 'redneck.'"

Do you?

Do you know that the overwhelming majority of white Southerners—well over 90% of them—never owned slaves even at the peak of slavery? Do you know that the term "redneck" dates all the way back to Scotland in the 1640s, when it was used to describe peasants who rebelled against the ruling class? Do you know that its most plausible American derivation is from the 1800s when it was used to describe those impoverished whites who didn't own slaves nor hire black sharecroppers and instead toiled in the fields and burned their pale necks red under the hot sun?

SPLC spokesmouth Maureen Costello, who heads a program called Teaching Tolerance, chided school officials: "Do no harm to a student's sense of identity. Everyone should feel welcome."

Everyone, that is, except poor white Southern rednecks. There's obviously no room at the lunch counter for them.

Black activist Jarrett Maupin II, a protégé of Al Sharpton who until recently sported one of those Sharptonesque Darth Vader hair helmets, filed a complaint about "Redneck Day" to a Denver office of the US Department of Education. In 2009 Maupin pleaded guilty to a felony count of making a false statement to the FBI. Maupin has also on at least one occasion spoken before an assembly of the Spiritual Israel Church and Its Army, a "largely African American" (read: "pretty much entirely African American") congregation that says prominent biblical figures from Adam all the way through Jesus were black.

In his letter to the Department of Education, Maupin claimed that Arizona's blacks—all ten or so of them—were "outraged over the controversial celebration" and that all students of all hues were "negatively impacted by the racially-insensitive theme."

On July 18, the DoE responded to Maupin with a letter:

> We have determined that we have the authority to investigate this allegation...the scope of OCR's investigation will be limited to whether a racially hostile environment was created due to language and actions that were not protected by the First Amendment.

Mind you, in 2012 a federal judge said it would be constitutional for Arizona's Hispanic students to sue the state for discontinuing "La Raza" studies that would by any objective measure be deemed intensely hostile and demeaning toward gringos.

But logical consistency has never intruded upon the increasingly insane Passion Play known as modern American race relations.

To me, the solution is simple. American blacks took the word "nigger" away from whites by "reclaiming" it, although technically it was never theirs in the first place. I suggest they do the same thing with the word "redneck" and the Rebel flag.

And we, as Americans, should achieve this cultural breakthrough the best way we know how: through a television show. I believe Hollywood should resurrect the classic TV program *The Dukes of Hazzard* with an all-black cast. Rather than running moonshine, the boys should evade the local authorities by peddling, oh, I don't know—crack cocaine? And they can "reclaim" the word "redneck" for themselves. They can even keep the Rebel flag on their pimped-out ride. And to make everyone happy and ensure that not a soul gets offended, they can call the show *The Spooks of Hazzard*.

26

Let's Hope the Next Bomber Is a Liberal Journalist

Observing the noxious media aftermath following the Boston Marathon bombings of April 2013, it has become abundantly clear that we, as a nation, need to start racially profiling liberal writers.

I first heard about the bombings from a little old white lady at a gas station down the street, and she said that "terrorists" were the likely culprits.

As someone who's increasingly bewitched and bewildered by the political use of semantics, I have severe misgivings about the word "terrorism." The US has been bombing massive swaths of the Middle East in varying degrees of intensity ever since the first Gulf War, which undoubtedly induces terror among the locals there, yet magically that's somehow not "terrorism." To me, "terrorism" is to "authorized military bombing" what a "cult" is to a "religion"—the main difference seems to be that neither the cults nor the terrorists have gone pro yet.

Even the most conscientiously objective among us have our biases, formed mostly by life experiences and where we find ourselves in the social pecking order. I find myself more suspicious of the major media and the US government than I do of either Muslims or rural redneck rubes, and when I got home from the gas station to read online that the bombings had occurred at the Boston Marathon, my first thought was of the 2010 British film *Four Lions*, where a quartet of bumbling jihadists blow themselves up at the London Marathon. But I didn't suspect Muslims as much as I suspected some pill-popping, attention-seeking, media-addled copycat.

And since the feds bleed what I presume are tens of billions from taxpayers such as myself to fund the CIA yet won't divulge exactly how much they're bleeding from us nor how they're spending that money, you can't shame me into silence by calling me a "paranoid conspiracy theorist" that I also wondered whether the bombings may have been a false-flag operation.

So although I had my suspicions, I reserved judg-ment, because that's what a journalist is *supposed* to do, or at least that's what they taught me in jour-nalism school before modern academia became entirely submerged in the ever-rising floodwaters of Cultural Marxism.

This wasn't the case with many other alleged jour-nalists. Those on the "right" tended to suspect Muslims, and those on the "left" were fairly wetting themselves with gleeful anticipation that it was one of those gun-toting, tax-resisting, rural Angry White Males that has served as their cultural "other" and chief movie villain for generations now.

Since I'm a white male and not a Muslim, I don't quite cotton to such rank defamation and stereo-typing.

Michael Moore stopped gnawing on his *Flint-stones*-sized rack of barbecued ribs long enough to note that being white would help you escape scrutiny as a bombing suspect. Moore would know something about being white, seeing as he owns a sprawling mansion in an area that is estimated to be 98% white and has *no* black residents.

Racial witch-hunter Tim Wise, who looks like the bastard love child of an albino beaver and Dr. Evil, allegedly lives in an area that is 97% white and 0% black, so he, too, ought to know a little about the "white privilege" against which he's constantly railing.

Wise kinda-sorta claims to be white in an apparent quest to score self-flagellation points, but not really, since he says his Jewish ancestors were only able to achieve success by slyly *passing* as white. So if I'm understanding him correctly, even though he insists he's white and that white guilt is a real thing, don't try to pin any the *bad* stuff about whiteness on him, because he's not really white. This, apparently, is how he's able to feel justified in plotting the "destruction" of the "conservative old white people [who] have pretty much always been the bad guys" while he refers to Jews as "my people."

Fuck me with a *dreidel* if that "destruction" line doesn't sound somewhat genocidal, Uncle Tim. But what the hell do I know—I'm rendered deaf, dumb, and blind by "white privilege," right?

Although the Boston bombings had nothing to do with whiteness, Wise immediately squirted his shopworn "white privilege" meme all over the blood and guts in Boston.

Picking up the bash-whitey baton from Tim Wise was David Sirota at salon.com, who signed his name to an article titled "Let's hope the Boston Marathon bomber is a white American." No, I'm not kidding. That was the title. After facing a ferocious backlash, Sirota doubled down and pissed out another screed called "I still hope the bomber is a white American" a day later.

In his first piece, the scrawny and apopleptic Sirota, who Wikipedia says "describes himself as 'a Jew'" and once worked for AIPAC, argued that unlike Muslims, white males are not perceived as an "existential threat," despite the fact that white males have endured a couple of generations of ceaseless stereotyping and outright collective blood libel at the hands of American media and academia.

I'm not sure why Jewish writers tend to treat Muslims far more gingerly than they do non-Jewish white males. Do they honestly think Muslims are fonder of Jews than white males are? Or is it that, unlike non-Jewish white males, Muslims tend to bite back? Whether it's primal fear, a misguided sense of compassion, or some cockeyed combination of the two, it appears that "Muslim privilege" rather than "white privilege" is what's at work in the leftist double standard.

Soon after the bombing, the FBI revealed the bombing suspects to be Chechen Muslims, who are technically Caucasian but not "white males" in the commonly understood pejorative sense.

I'm no fan of Muslims and I also understand there has been a civilizational clash between the Islamic world and what's known as "Christendom" ever since Muhammad started slaying everything in his path and bedding preteens. But it seems as if modern jihadist bombings only started in earnest after Zionists started bombing what was once known as Palestine in their quest to establish Israel. So why is it that when we think of terrorist bombers, it's either McVeigh or bin Laden and never the Stern Gang? And why do leftist bombers wind up with tenure at prestigious universities?

Could it be that the leftist media downplays, or even ignores, such acts of terrorism because that part of the media is egregiously stacked with a wildly disproportionate quotient of a specific minority Who Must Never Be Named Under Threat of Eternal Damnation? Perish the thought! (My Jew-sniffing dog sometimes makes mistakes, and it's not as if Americans of that ancestry always advertise their heritage, but to the best of my research skills I counted anywhere from 13 to 19 "chosen" peeps from the 25 luminaries on a list of prominent leftist media pundits, which would comprise 52%-79% of the total and thus a whopping statistical overrepresentation of anywhere from

2,600% to 3,950%. And there's not one black person on that list. Holy mackerel, Andy!)

Is it a mortal sin to question why those who never zip their lips about trash-compacting "diversity" into every nook and cranny of American life tend to come from a tiny and stubbornly non-diverse demographic?

Maybe if you'd been able to restrain yourselves from endlessly screaming about the unique evil of white people, I wouldn't have started to look into exactly who was doing most of the screaming. Since you apparently can't help yourself from continually profiling me, don't cry foul when I start profiling you. And I don't think it qualifies as imagining there are Jews in your sandwich when anywhere from half to three-quarters of the hoagie you're feeding me is stuffed with kosher meat.

Palefaced XY-chromosome devils have been persistently framed in popular discourse as eternal oppressors and congenital spewers of venom, bile, and hatred. But despite everything the media has been peddling for generations, it appears that this oft-maligned demographic suffers from a fatal flaw, one that runs contrary to the stereotype—they're *way too nice*. They're not homicidally intolerant so much as they're suicidally tolerant. And unless their antagonists—whether they're self-loathing crackers such as Michael Moore or anyone else in the increasingly hostile and jeering Rainbow Coalition—learn to cool it with the screaming, it appears that the only option is to start screaming back. Otherwise it seems evident that the tireless bashers of everything white and male don't view white males as a powerful oppressor so much as an easy target.

27

Why, Oh Why Is Iowa So Iowhite?

On New Year's Day 2012, NBC honking head Andrea Mitchell tried making America hip to the Hawkeye State's unforgivable lack of hipness:

> *The rap on Iowa: it doesn't represent the rest of the country—too white, too evangelical, too rural.*

This isn't the first time Ms. Mitchell—presumably a reporter rather than some wacked-out urban-supremacist sockpuppet—has made such a statement. In 2008 she chuckled while wondering why Barack Obama would bother to campaign in Southwest Virginia:

> *This is real [laughs] redneck, sort of, um, bordering on Appalachia country.*

Mitchell's recent comments about Iowa echo those made by *New York Times* publisher Arthur "Pinch" Sulzberger in a December 17 column:

> *Iowa has long been criticized as too much of an outlier to be permanently endowed such an outsize influence in shaping the presidential field. Too small, critics say. Too rural. Too white.*

Iowa ranks 26th in the USA for area and 30th for population, so rather than being "too small," it's pretty average. We're also not sure what's meant by "too rural," but it apparently means that 61% urban simply isn't urban enough for snooty coast-huggers such as Sulzberger and Mitchell. And the *Washington Examiner* recently cited a Pew survey pegging Iowa as slightly less evangelical than the national norm. So in truth, Iowa isn't all that freakishly small, evangelical, or rural.

Which leaves us with "too white."

While Mitchell and Sulzberger were careful not to call Iowa "too white" themselves—they used such responsibility-deflecting phrases as "the rap on" and "critics say"—we've yet to see them depict Mississippi as "too black" or the relatively tiny isle of Manhattan—where, as luck would have it, Sulzberger, Mitchell, and her husband, ex-Federal Reserve Chairman Alan Greenspan were all born—as being too, you know, "Armenian" or whatever.

This ain't to say that Iowa ain't white. The state is currently around 91% white—not terribly different than America as a whole was in 1960. But by modern standards, it's now a little *extra*-white. Compared to the current national average (63.7% in 2010) Iowa is roughly "over-white" to the same degree that New York City is "under-white" (33% in 2010).

Washington Post writer Courtland Milloy—a black man whose skin tone is somewhat over-white compared to the national Black Mean Hue, not that we ever notice such things—recently found Iowa to be far too white for his tastes:

> *I noticed that nearly everybody was white: white people smiling over coffee, white people applauding at candidate forums, white people singing praise songs at church.*

Why, it sounds like the apocalypse!

On the opposite end of the Terror Spectrum are those who make it clear they think the state's too white by roving in packs and beating the shit out of white people at the Iowa State Fair.

But as we've been repeatedly lectured, we live in a post-racial society, so the possibility that certain elements of the overwhelmingly urban-based mainstream media have some sort of "anti-white, anti-rural" agenda is a laughable notion that only retarded toothless inbred pale-skinned ghostfaced crackers who live in the boondocks would ever believe.

Obviously we can't trust anyone in the media to say what they actually mean, so when they say Iowa is "too white," we must assume that they are speaking in code.

Maybe they really mean it's too German.

Maybe they secretly mean it's a very safe place where there can be massive flooding without massive rioting. Maybe they mean it was recently rated the eighth-safest state and the sixth-best state in which to live. Or maybe not, because then they'd have to concede that the states rated as even better and safer—places such as New Hampshire, Vermont, Maine, the Dakotas, and Wyoming—were themselves almost unconscionably white.

Maybe they want people to know about Iowa's economy. It has one of the nation's lowest unemployment rates, and the few states with even lower rates are, well, mighty-tighty-whitey themselves. Comparing income to the cost of living, sweet li'l Des Moines is the USA's richest urban area.

Maybe they feel that Iowa has been unfairly stereotyped as a breeding ground of superstitious illiterate cornfield bumpkins. In reality, Iowa has been one of the most literate states in America for 100 years and running. Iowa students are said to "consistently lead the nation in standardized achievement-test scores." A government website claims that 93 percent of Iowa's schools perform above the national average. Iowa ranks third when it comes to libraries per resident. It also has one of the nation's lowest high-school dropout rates. To be fair, not all of Iowa's schools perform so well. To be fairer, these schools tend to be in areas that few would describe as "too white."

So when they say Iowa is "too white," perhaps what they really mean is that it's too safe, too economically stable, and far too literate to adequately represent mainstream America—especially the "mainstream America" they have planned for us.

I agree. Iowa is definitely too white.

28

Give the Bigots a Pill

Get in line, all ye racists—they have a pill for you now.

Several supposedly respectable websites erupted in a blinding sun shower of bigot-hating joy at a 2012 Oxford University study involving a common blood-pressure pill called Propranolol. Headlines said the study proves the pill "reduces in-built racism," "Makes People Less Racist," and even has the spiritual potential to "open hearts and minds."

As a friend of mine asked, "What's next: an enema that cures homophobia?"

The study, "Propranolol reduces implicit negative racial bias," was recently published in *Psychopharmacology*, and all the Tribbles on the Starship Equality are purring with glee at the idea that science has FINALLY found a pill to cure the evil racist scourge. Online comments sounded happy little bugles at the advent of a Brave New Progressive World in which Propranolol replaces Soma:

> *This pill should be mandatory for all right-wing Republicans, tea bags, KKK, people who hate the immigrants and want them deported, etc. What a much better world this would be.*

> *Let's put Propanolol in the water supply and stamp out the ugliness of Republicanism forever.*

> *Stop being so paranoid, and take a chill pill. So what if the white race are wiped out.*

> *There's already a pill to cure racists, it contains cyanide ?*

Ironically, Propranolol was developed by a Scottish scientist whose surname was Black. The pill appears to target brain areas that regulate fear, making that lion who's stealthfully creeping toward you seem like a furry little pussycat.

The recent Oxford study regarding the pill's ability to reduce "racism"—a social construct which to this day no one has been able to define to my satisfaction—was based on an unforgivably tiny sample of 36 participants, only 18 of whom received the Propranolol while the other 18 took placebos. Displaying what perhaps is egregious explicit racial and gender bias, researchers selected only white males as their guinea pigs.

In summarizing her study's results, lead author Sylvia Terbeck said something that resonated with me emotionally:

> Implicit racial bias can occur even in people with a sincere belief in equality.

Hey, I think that's happened to me, too. Even though I sincerely wanted to believe people are equal, something inside me told me that they aren't. So now there's a pill for that? I simply pop a pill in my mouth, and everything's erased?

The researchers noted that the pill had no effect on "explicit" racism, a presumably measurable object they measured by giving the participants a questionnaire regarding how "warm" one feels toward ethnic groups and left/right politics in general. Researchers conceded that the "dominance of political norms of equality and tolerance in Western democracies limits the overt expression of prejudice"—in other words, publicly expressing "racist" views threatens the prevailing political power structure and is almost universally considered to be a thought crime.

The study's observed differences were all in the mystically mossy realm of "implicit" racism, which supposedly measures one's subconscious bigotry by making you play a rapid-fire online game.

High-paid anti-racist witch hunters get blisters on their feet walking coast to coast trying to find evidence of discrimination and overt racial hatred these days. Yet despite the lack of visible barriers, they note—accurately—that not everyone in society is performing equally. So they insist that such "disparate impact" is caused by fundamental unfairness rather than something as screamingly obvious as disparate ability.

So rather than wasting their time waiting for that next Alabama lynching that never seems to come, they've decided to look *inside* you. They're peeking inside your heart, even though you didn't ask. It doesn't matter that your behavior causes zero literal harm to other races; they're going to find a way to prove you're a racist, anyway.

And if you resist, well, that's all the proof they need.

The yardstick these "scientists" wield to measure the evil that lurks within your heart is known as the Implicit Association Test (IAT), brought to you by our friends at Harvard, home to such eminently Caucasian-friendly personages as Noel Ignatiev and Derrick Bell.

You can take the test online. You're instructed to plow through it as fast as possible—this will tap into your "subconscious" mind. You use your left and right fingers to make selections while white and black faces along with positive and negative words (e.g., "Happy," "Sad," "Glorious," "Awful") flash before your eyes. They'll switch the "good" and "evil" words back and forth between the "European American" and "African American" sides, and your reaction time supposedly measures how rapidly you associate good and evil words with each side. The assumption is that if you quickly associate evil words with the black side, you're prejudiced against them rather than, oh, the former victim of an armed robbery at the hands of five black assailants.

I took the test five times without chemically altering myself for the duration. Twice the results said I favored whites, twice they said I favored blacks, and once it said I'm neutral. If I'd decided to, say, pop a black-market Quaalude halfway through the testing and waited until it kicked in, the results could have been even more skewed and I may have wound up simultaneously loving and hating everyone. And this is the "science" they're using.

But even making the shaky assumption that the tests are accurate, some studies using the IAT yielded results that may not please progressive researchers' fluffy golden ears. One of them concluded that whites were more color-blind—i.e., less "racist"—than blacks and Latinos. Another showed that physicians who scored as more "biased" in the IAT tests actually tended to discriminate less in practice than supposedly unbiased ones. One study's results suggested that in day-to-day life, blacks preferred to interact with whites whom the IAT had categorized as "highly racially biased" than with whites who weren't. Another study claimed the IAT is fundamentally flawed because its results seemed to be based more on simple cognitive inertia at speeding through all those flashing faces and words.

In short: This recent Oxford study is worthless.

What deserves further study is a fairly recent leftist trend to eagerly dive into the murky waters of the Eugenics Ocean provided that the "science" can somehow prove that they are biologically different than their thought-villain nemeses on the right. After rolling their eyes, holding their noses, and chanting "la-la-la-la" at any studies that appeared to establish innate racial differences, they are now wrapping their slender pink tentacles around any study—no matter how dubious its methodology—that suggests leftist egalitarians are almost a different race than their ideological enemies. After decades of claiming they'd eternally discredited what they called "scientific racism," they are launching forward with a new academic discipline I'll call "scientific anti-racism." Or maybe "totalitarian liberal eugenics." Or maybe I'm still working on its name.

Leftists shrieked like happy hamsters at a recent Canadian (of course) study linking "prejudice" and "right-wing" ideology to "lower cognitive ability." They also squealed like shiny baby piglets at another recent study that purported to show that liberals and conservatives (whatever that means) have different brain structures.

And though they claim to celebrate the rainbow of differences that Goddess has bequeathed us, somehow they find room in their wide-open minds to cheer for the day when we breed all of those differences into extinction. Neither will these diversicrats tolerate any true diversity of thought—they're lurching toward Soviet-style political psychiatry by suggesting that ideological disagreement on racial matters is a mental disorder requiring medication.

Sound paranoid? I'm sure they're working on a pill for *that*, too.

Sanity is in many ways a social construct, one that varies widely from society to society. In a pragmatic sense I'll admit it's crazy to go against the crowd, however abjectly deluded and brainwashed that crowd may be. If you don't run with them, they'll stomp right over you like wild buffalo.

Despite the soul-blotting excesses of Soviet and Maoist totalitarianism, many neo-Marxists still appear to believe that the control freaks and power psychos are confined to the right.

How about we work on a pill that cures extreme partisan psychosis?

Or one that cures stupidity? Lotta that going around.

I haven't dabbled in science since that seventh-grade project I did with the snails, but it's obvious to me that "social science" is anything but a science. This new anti-racism snake oil they're peddling is an unholy amalgamation of soft eugenics and punitive psychiatry. The Two Joes—Mengele and Stalin—are shaking hands inside a tiny little heart pill. Pop it in your mouth and smile.

29

Attack of the Killer Racist Peanuts

There is no longer a need for satire these days because the world ridicules itself. Modern American culture is a self-parody set on autopilot.

The latest round of nuttiness involves public education and peanut butter. The humble peanut, you see, has become politicized. It is now a "hate food." The peanut defiantly blocks school entrances, standing in the way of a progressive *putsch* to enable American schoolchildren to become as physically and culturally hypersensitive as possible.

Two recent news stories—one involving a contraband peanut-butter-and-jelly sandwich at an Arkansas school and the other revolving around a rotund, buffalo-faced Oregon grade-school principal who fingers peanut-butter sandwiches as emblems of "white privilege"—illustrate that our public schools are filled to the rafters with nuts who are severely allergic to reality.

In the peanut-sized town of Viola, Arkansas, a teacher confiscated a boy's PB&J sandwich as if it was a hand grenade and sent a stern letter to the young lad's parents explaining a school policy designed to protect a micro-minority of students afflicted with peanut allergies. This inflamed the passions of local pro-peanut parents, who launched a "School Nut Ban Discussion" group on Facebook. The kernel of the matter involves whether the "rights" of a tiny minority of peanut-averse children override those of the vast majority of kids who enjoy this high-protein, low-cost staple of the American diet.

Full disclosure: I grew up gorging on Gaucho peanut-butter cookies, Fluffernutters, Peanut Butter Kandy Kakes, and my Aunt Berle's *nonpareil* peanut-butter fudge. I still enjoy the occasional Southern-styled boiled peanut and nurse a mild-to-intense skepticism about "peanut allergies," which were unheard-of during my beardless youth.

So when I hear that some children can now die merely from *smelling* peanuts and that adults are filing race-and-disability-discrimination lawsuits hinging on their skin color and peanut sensitivities, I wax somewhat peanut-defensive.

Children with peanut allergies, whether real or imagined, have become the homosexuals of alternative culinary lifestyles and are said to suffer severe social ostracism and even bullying. If their school isn't progressive enough to ban peanuts entirely, these hapless youngsters are often segregated in "Nut-Free Zones," tiny dietary Warsaw Ghettos that highlight their difference and cultural otherness. This cripples their self-esteem, and even though there's evidence that self-esteem and academic performance may be *inversely* correlated, the trained seals of modern public education never stop barking about how higher self-esteem is the cornerstone of higher learning.

Although peanut allergies aren't entirely the nutty figments of soccer moms' imaginations, a study in England found that four of five kids who thought they suffered from food allergies were merely trained hypochondriacs. There's been a documented rise in peanut allergies, but the cause remains elusive. Such allergies are virtually nonexistent in Third World countries where kids face constant exposure to dirt and bacteria. One study found that peanut allergies are less prevalent in children who've been exposed to peanuts at a young age, suggesting that a fanatically sanitized, overprotective approach to child rearing may contribute to oversensitive kids with underperforming immune systems. So by trying to protect kids *from* everything, modern parents may actually be making their children more susceptible *to* everything.

Portland grade-school principal Verenice Gutierrez, whose bloated frame suggests she's scarfed down two dozen peanut-butter sandwiches every day of her life, is clearly susceptible to Cultural Marxist indoctrination and appears determined to break down young Portlanders' immunity to it.

Gutierrez—whose surname begins with the word "Gut"—presides over a school whose academic performance ranks in the state's lowest fifteen percent, a dubious honor shared by other Portland schools that, as luck would have it, are named after Cesar Chavez and Rosa Parks.

Although the school recently lost some full-time teachers due to budget cuts, the Portland school district reportedly saw fit to fork over more than a half-million dollars to indoctrinate its teachers about how "white privilege"—rather than, say, low IQs, laziness, or widespread cultural allergies to assimilating—is the culprit for low academic achievement at her school, which is only one-quarter white.

Gutierrez, whom a *Portland Tribune* writer described as possessing the magical power to hear "the subtle language of racism every day," says that peanut-butter-and-jelly sandwiches invidiously discriminate against "Somali or Hispanic students, who might not eat sandwiches." She apparently hasn't considered that these kids may be *extremely* privileged by dint of the fact that they don't live in Somalia or Mexico.

When confronted with the fact that a parent complained that Gutierrez permits a drum club at the school whose membership is open only to black and Hispanic males, she scoffed and said:

> *When white people do it, it is not a problem, but if it's for kids of color, then it's a problem? Break it down for me. That's your white privilege and your whiteness.*

I was unaware that American whites, especially schoolchildren, are permitted to "do it" at all, but if they did attempt to form any school-sponsored organization open exclusively to whites, it would not only be a "problem," it'd be a headline-grabbing national scandal. Such is the state of modern "white privilege."

Gutierrez appears to believe that this invisible "white privilege" is the reason why "students of color" aren't doing well in American schools, ignoring the fact that when left to their own devices, members of *la raza* aren't exactly engines of innovation. (To be fair, the ancient Incas are credited with being peanut butter's pioneers.)

Still, Gutierrez has resolutely tossed her formidable bulk behind the idea that the only way for Hispanic students to bridge the school-achievement gap is to Hispanically build a Hispanicist interpretation of their Hispanicity. During her tenure at another Portland public school, Gutierrez was involved with a group called Future Hispanic Leaders. On a 17-minute video, she spoke of fomenting "pride of culture, pride of heritage, and pride of language" to "empower" Hispanic students to feel "that they belong with others who look just like them." On that video, you can actually hear her off-camera as she coaches young Hispanistudents about how feeling kinship with *la raza* helps them do their schoolwork and how society encourages everyone to view white students as "perfect."

Quetzalcoatl forbid that she would ever ask them to focus on reading, writing, and arithmetic.

Ms. Gutierrez, you are the turd in the punchbowl of American education.

I'm going to excuse myself. I have to throw up.

Then I'm going to eat a peanut-butter sandwich.

30

Can't We All Just Get Post-Racial?

In 2008, a starry-eyed, hopeful, and fatally credulous nation elected Barack Obama to the presidency based largely on some dimwitted notion that he would usher us into a glittering new "post-racial" era where everyone got along, had group orgies, and joyously mixed their genes into a highly agreeable shade of caramel.

Four years later, "researchers" seem perplexed that the nation is just a tad more "racist" than it was four years ago.

A recently released "study" co-sponsored by the Associated Press—which, smack my ivory-colored ass if I'm wrong, is supposed to dispassionately report facts rather than issue studies that treat indefinable terms such as "prejudice" as if they were remotely scientific—has concluded that Americans are a whopping three percent more "prejudiced" than they were in 2008.

Here's the punch line, served straight with no chaser by the objective fact-diggers at the AP:

> *Racial attitudes have not improved in the four years since the United States elected its first black president, an Associated Press poll finds, as a majority of Americans now express prejudice toward blacks whether they recognize those feelings or not.*

Unless you want to be culturally stigmatized forever, don't you dare question the study's methodology, which concluded that it was "prejudiced" to respond in the affirmative when asked whether blacks tend to be more violent. Shut your eyes and ignore the facts, or we'll bludgeon you into submission with nasty names. Because we all know that despite what all the evidence suggests, what you're displaying is prejudice rather than postjudice. Even after decades of what may be hard personal experience, you are obviously prejudging.

And kindly snap your mind shut from wondering why it isn't "racist" that 96% of blacks voted for Obama in 2008 or that Mitt Romney's support among blacks hovered around 0%. We can only hope that Obama is reelected and uses his unparalleled skills at unifying and healing to help black Americans finally get over Romney's unfortunate skin color. Obviously it's the Republicans who are alienating nonwhites, and the Democrats' ceaseless white-bashing could not possibly be driving whites away in droves.

The ominous warning of the AP study is that this new upsurge in "prejudice" could cost Obama the election. So don't blame them if disillusioned Obamabots riot as a result. Clearly it would not be the fault of his supporters, nor of the race-baiters in the media and the race "experts" in academia—the blame will lie solely at the freckled feet of the "prejudiced."

Don't blame black pundits—who make a living by being black and talking about their blackness and how hard it is to be black—for stoking racial tension. Don't blame the ones who see no irony of accusing Romney of "playing the race card" while their own words appear under a banner that says "East Central Florida's Black Voice." Don't blame those who talk about "the childishness of some whites" or that Romney, by not even mentioning race, was somehow contributing to "the niggerization" of Obama.

Don't blame white pundits who talk about "coded speech" and "dog whistles," those who blame everything on "racial hatred" and urge a default editorial strategy of "call them racists."

Don't blame a media that never shuts the hell up about race, whether it involves the "Colorectal Cancer Racial Gap," how racism may cause weight gain, or whether your baby is a racist. Don't blame a media that works in cahoots with law enforcement to foster the impression that no matter how savage, deliberate, or merciless a black-on-white attack is—even if the perpetrators taunted their victims with racial epithets during the assault—it hardly ever seems to be labeled anything beyond a "possible" hate crime.

And we'll jolt your nipples with cables attached to a car battery if you're foolhardy enough to wonder if it might partially be Obama's fault that after four years in office, Americans are a bit more "racist" instead of full-blown post-racial. Don't blame him for being the candidate who made a point of his race in 2008, all under the slippery guise of predicting his opponent would make a point of his race. Don't blame him for beseeching Hispanics to help him "punish our enemies." Don't blame him for dishonoring his white mother and the white grandparents who raised him for the fact that he described himself as exclusively "black" on his Census form. Don't blame him for selecting an Attorney General who is absurdly biased in racial matters. Don't blame him for presuming the white cop was at fault in the arrest of Henry Louis Gates. And don't blame him for exploiting a racially charged killing by saying that if he "had a son, he'd look like Trayvon."

And don't for a second think that perhaps many well-meaning whites are finally growing a little defensive after realizing that trying hard not to be "racist" is the most thankless job of all. Brush from your consciousness any suggestion that no matter how open-minded and compassionate you try to be, it never seems to be enough. Don't dare contemplate that many Americans have reached Peak Guilt and will start refusing to fit any more guilt into their already guilt-addled bodies. Don't think about the idea that tribalism may be a natural instinct and that trying to go "post-racial" is as absurd as trying to go "post-sexual." If you entertain such notions for even a second, it's obvious that you're prejudiced. And now we have tests that can prove it.

31

The Spit-Roasting of Paula Deen

Deep-battered and Southern-fried celebrity chef Paula Deen is crying tears made of butter after admitting in a court deposition that a long, long time ago she said the word "nigger."

The story became yet another tedious and barf-inducing racial scandal in 2013. It led to the Food Channel, where the cheesecake-fryin', nut-droppin' Georgia porker had ruled the pigsty for over a decade, announcing that they would not renew Deen's contract because, well, c'mon, she said the word "nigger" and that's the modern equivalent of the unpardonable sin.

Amid all the public shirt-rending, the wagging of fingers and shaking of heads, the tut-tutting and tsk-tsking, the eyeball-pluckingly pious denunciations about shamefulness, evil, heinousness, and raw pure unabashed hateful unforgivable Southern wickedness, it mostly escaped notice that Deen (an Obama supporter) said she'd used the word in a discussion with her husband after a black man held a gun to her head while robbing her at the bank where she worked.

We live in a topsy-turvy world where people are far more offended if someone *says* "nigger" than if they *act* like one. Thus, the sentencing of three black Marines who murdered a fellow white Marine and his black wife received almost zero notice in the national press.

Deen's deposition involved a lawsuit filed by a white woman named Lisa Jackson, a former employee at Uncle Bubba's Oyster House in Savannah, GA. The "Bubba" in question is Deen's brother, Earl "Bubba" Hiers, who is variously accused in the complaint of drinking hard liquor from a paper cup, calling blacks "monkeys," saying that Obama should have come down South to "nigger-rig" the Gulf oil spill, saying he wished he could send all his black workers on a boat back to Africa, forbidding black workers from using the restaurant's front entrance, telling off-color jokes, surfing for porn, and basically doing everything one might suspect a guy named "Bubba" of doing.

Jackson also claims that when she asked Deen (who has been held in contempt of court for refusing to fork over a video that allegedly depicts her simulating fellatio on a chocolate éclair) what sort of outfits she'd prefer to see her black workers wearing, she received the following response:

> Well what I would really like is a bunch of little niggers to wear long-sleeve white shirts, black shorts and black bow ties, you know in the Shirley Temple days, they used to tap dance around.

In Deen's subsequent deposition, the most infamous passage—apart from Deen unabashedly saying "of course" when asked if she'd ever used "the N-word"—involved wedding plans for Bubba that involved strictly black servants garbed in formal attire. Deen said that such plans never came to fruition because she feared someone might "misinterpret" her intentions.

Naturally, the bloodthirsty progressive press misinterpreted and misrepresented her intentions. Various accounts lent the impression that she had actually hired black workers to dress as slaves.

The backlash was as quick and ferocious as these things tend to be these days, and Deen quickly cobbled together a very inept video apology and then a slightly less inept video apology.

But to baser creatures, apologies are usually inter-
preted as weakness, and we all know how wolf
packs treat weakness.

On CNN, a gay Jewish man named Howard Brag-
man relished Deen's downfall in a manner that was
borderline psychotic:

> And the day she dies, this will be in her obituary. She has
> to wear the stain the rest of her life and she's earned it.

Bragnan also said that "words hurt" and "damage
people," although I doubt he was referring to Paula
Deen and her hundreds of suddenly unemployed
underlings, who were all *literally* hurt not by a
word's usage but by the sanctimonious lynch mob
that reacted to it.

In a rant reeking of anti-*goyishe* animus, sports
writer Dan Bernstein calls Deen an "Ugly Racist"
who peddles "lowbrow, redneck garbage" and
indulges in "downright inhuman behavior" while
appealing to "diabetic simpletons." Apparently able
to read minds, he states it as a "fact" that "Paula
Deen just flatly, clearly, undeniably views blacks as
lesser people, if entirely human at all."

Clearly, Dan Bernstein views white Southern non-
Jewish rednecks as entirely human.

The *Christian Science Monitor* glumly pondered whether it was possible to say anything positive about Southern history and cuisine without conjuring the smelly taint of bigotry, hatred, hateful bigotry, and bigoted hatefulness.

A writer for the yay-for-blacks blog The Root lamented that instead of taking his advice to "Bash Deen" as humorlessly as possible, younger blacks (and a sprinkling of crackers) on Twitter had a bit of fun speculating about some of her favorite dishes such as "Honey Bunches of Ropes," "Porch Monkey Bread," "Colored Greens," "Klu [sic] Klux Flan," "Cotton Pickin' Fried Chicken," and my personal favorite, "Lynchables."

Both Salon and Mediaite, which you'd expect to be cynical toward primitively mystical notions of morality—or at least Christian ones—referred to Deen's "sin."

What a preposterously magical and mystical word "nigger" has become. I think back to the O. J. Simpson murder trial—probably the most high-profile legal proceeding in the past quarter-century—where defense lawyers turned the jury's attention away from a brutal double slaying to whether a policeman had said the word "nigger."

No matter what the powers that be insist, no matter how hard they try to purge it from one of American literature's greatest works, it really is nothing more than a word. It only has the power that you superstitious morons give to it.

I also think of the futility when a white person apologizes for uttering it. Paula Deen's downfall isn't the first time a public figure publicly groveled to no avail after it was revealed that they'd said "nigger." Offering a tearful, shell-shocked apology didn't do Duane "Dog the Bounty Hunter" Chapman or Michael "Kramer" Richards any good, either.

So I suggest an entirely different tack, one more along the lines of "Draw a Cartoon of Muhammad Day." The only way to strip the word of the "power" that people insist it has is for everyone to start saying it as often as possible. I suspect the only thing that will stop this insanity is for everyone to start saying the word *en masse* like a sudden populist upsurge of racial Tourette's. Let it burst forth like an epidemic of niggerrhea. Throw the word right back in the faces of the pious turds who use it to destroy careers through cowardly festivals of public shaming. I'm only half-joking when I suggest that the only rational solution for this ceaselessly embarrassing national moral panic is for people to start filming themselves saying the word "nigger" and posting it online.

32

Softly Wiping the Chalk From the Blackboard

The 15th annual White Privilege Conference recently ended in Madison, WI. As is usually the case with the locales for such public displays of white ethnomasochism, Madison's quotient of blacks is roughly half the national average. In contrast, presumably ignorant and "prejudiced" white Southerners—the kind of people most despised by bourgeois-yet-Marxist whites who believe in fairy tales such as "white privilege"—have for centuries lived in the blackest part of the nation. It is typically whites with the *least* amount of experience living alongside blacks that tend to idolize colored folks beyond all reason.

I had initially planned to attend the event as a sort of performance art—dressed head-to-toe in white with an entourage of Madison's white bikers drop-

ping me off and picking me up from each day's festivities—but alas, my white privilege was not so
extensive that I was able to afford the financial and
temporal sacrifices my attendance would have
required.

According to conference founder Eddie Moore, Jr.,
"white supremacy, white privilege, racism and
other forms of oppression are designed for your
destruction—designed to kill you." If that's the
case, privileged whites are doing a piss-poor job,
seeing as how the 400,000 or so Africans who were
transported to North America in slave ships
have—through the noxious evils of white privilege,
white technology, and living amid a predominantly
white culture—blossomed into around 40 million
modern American blacks. That's an increase of
100-1 and truly the most inept genocide in world
history.

I could be wrong, but at least judging from pictures
taken at the event, most of the attendees, local
hosts, and T-shirt models appeared to be white,
although I'd bet they'd say "whiteness" is a social
construct all while accepting guilt (and perhaps pri-
vate S&M whippings) for the idea that they benefit
from "white privilege" even though whiteness is
nothing more than an idea. Assuming they have
brains, how do they keep them from exploding?

A Wisconsin reporter estimates that the conference at minimum cost taxpayers $20,000 to further indoctrinate already brainwashed educators that white taxpayers are beastly, innately exploitive fanged vampires who deserve extinction.

Workshops during the four-day extravaganza included "White American Islamophobia," "White Privilege and the Color of Wealth," "Death of the Strong Black Sista," "How Do We Talk About Privilege, For Real?" "Against the Tea Party Movement," "White Women's Guide to Teaching Black Boys," and "Beyond Kumbaya: Promoting Privilege Discussions on College Campuses." Film screenings included such cinematic thought-turds as *The N!GGA Word*, *What Makes Me White*, and *The New Black*.

Apparently the only way to dismantle white privilege and usher in this long-promised and long-delayed era of post-racial harmony is to be absolutely fucking *obsessed* with race.

Phenotypically white professor Joe Feagin, past president of the American Sociology Association and author of *Living With Racism and White Racism* as well as roughly ten million other books about how white people are racist meanies, came dressed in his trademark sexy bolo tie. He purportedly claimed that all white people are either racists or "recovering racists" and allegedly uttered things such as "The white racial frame is more than cognitive. It's hostile, vicious, emotional, and visual," "Whites live the white racial frame like goldfish in a bowl of water," and "The heart of the white racial frame is white virtue/superiority. This is (unsurprisingly) the hardest thing for white people to see."

Feagin allegedly closed his speech with words from Martin Luther King and a photo of black American runners famously giving the Black Power salute at the 1968 Olympics in Mexico City. How urban and edgy of him!

What's easy for me to see—and unlike Joe Feagin, I don't wear glasses, rose-colored or otherwise—is that Joe Feagin is a white man suffering the late stages of Passover Syndrome.

Scanning the sponsors listed in the center column of the WPC's home page reveals a multicolored cornucopia of logos from likeminded churches and colleges. I don't attend church, so it is the colleges that I—to lift a ubiquitous progressive buzzword—find "problematic." Why are such absurd and absolutely unscientific medieval guilt scenarios—where "whiteness" is reduced to "evil" and Europeans' lopsidedly abundant contributions to science, art, and global longevity are either ignored or fraudulently dismissed as thievery from other cultures—being injected like mind-numbing psy-chiatric drugs into children's brains?

Behold passages from the conference's "Youth Action Project" page:

> • *Students will SEE and be fully aware of the multiple manifestations of white supremacy, white privilege, and other forms of oppression.*
> • *Students will have the courage and confidence to NAME white supremacy, white privilege, and other forms of oppression.*
> • *Students will ACT by taking effective, creative, and urgent measures to dismantle white supremacy, white privilege, and other forms of oppression.*
> • *Students will PROCEED as leaders, planting ongoing seeds of change.*

Apparently teaching students to READ and WRITE and ADD and SUBTRACT are no longer priorities. No, you have to *constantly* teach them—at least the white ones—*not* to be racist, which tends to undermine the oft-parroted canard that children need to be taught TO be racist.

So which one is it? If white kids need to be bitch-slapped from grades one through sixteen with the idea that white "racism" is bad, that would suggest they'd fall back into instinctual tribalism the moment you quit browbeating them. Your tirelessly aggressive indoctrination schemes imply a deep-seated insecurity about whether your beliefs are natural or have to be force-fed through tireless governmental, corporate, media, and religious brainwashing.

The only good idea that seemed to emerge from this farcical pink-pig hog-sloppin' guilt-fest came via a tweet from a conference attendee: "maybe we should stop giving black boys to white women teachers."

I think that's a capital idea, especially if the white women teachers are the typical self-loathing breed so prevalent these days—and by that I mean they hate the "white" part of themselves rather than the "female" part. I don't even think you need to set any new policies to make this a reality. If you keep pounding the idea that "whiteness = evil" into the skulls of the nation's increasingly nonwhite student population, those melanin-rich young'uns will eventually demand that white men and women stop teaching them altogether. Purely by delicious accident, white teachers will wind up softly erasing themselves like so much chalk from the blackboard.

33

Exiled to Racistville

Late one night in the summer of 2014, radio host Anthony Cumia nearly became the Bernie Goetz of shock jocks. But unlike Goetz, he didn't use his gun, even though he says he was carrying one when he was assaulted. Instead, he went on Twitter and ran his mouth after it happened. As a result, he lost his satellite radio gig and, presumably, the $3 million yearly salary that goes along with it.

Cumia, the cohost of *The Opie and Anthony Show*—which has been broadcasting in various incarnations for nearly twenty years and until this event happened had been running on Sirius XM Radio—says that after midnight on July 2, 2014, a black female approached him and punched him repeatedly under some scaffolding near Times Square. Cumia says he was out taking pictures—he's allegedly a photography geek—when he captured a shot of the woman walking under the scaffolding. She's framed almost in the center of the photo, so it would seem that she didn't accidentally wind up in the shot.

According to Cumia, the woman saw him snap the photo, indignantly stomped up to him, called him a "white motherfucker," and belted him in the face. On Twitter shortly after the incident, Cumia wrote that he replied by calling her a "&$;;-:"—since it's six characters and the middle two characters are repeated, I'm going to way out on the banana-tree limb and assume he means "nigger"—whereupon she punched him five more times. Cumia says that about five black males then started hassling him.

He seems to have extricated himself from the situation without any significant loss of blood, at which point he went into full-on Charles Bronson/Clint Eastwood/Travis Bickle mode in the middle of the night on Twitter:

> *It's really open season on white people in this day and age. No recourse. Fight back and you're a racist. The predators know this. Good luck....They run things now. We're done....There's a deep seeded [sic] problem with violence in the black community. Try to address it and you'll be exiled to racistville. But it's real.*

As far as I can tell, the term "shock jock" refers to any broadcaster who says things that no one would have found shocking 50 years ago. Though Cumia has buttered his bread for two decades as one of the country's better known "shock jocks," Cumia's lava-belching Twitter tirade proved too shocking for his employer:

> SiriusXM has terminated its relationship with Anthony Cumia of the Opie & Anthony channel. The decision was made, and Cumia informed, late Thursday, July 3 after careful consideration of his racially charged and hate-filled remarks on social media. Those remarks and postings are abhorrent to SiriusXM, and his behavior is wholly inconsistent with what SiriusXM represents.

But Cumia is far more than merely the latest celebrity victim of the ongoing Great Anti-Racist Purge. What adds an entirely different dimension to his case is the alleged real-life violence. At the time of this writing, his purported Negress assailant has yet to emerge to tell her side, but if Cumia's not lying, his firing and one-way boat ticket to Racistville are evidence that in modern America, it's considered worse for white people to say or think bad things about blacks than it is for blacks to physically assault whites. I suspect that Cumia drew more wrath upon himself for daring to mention black-on-white violence than he did for using words such as "cunt" and even the time-honored "nigger." Acknowledging blacks' overwhelming edge in American interracial-violence statistics these days is one of the things you can't say if you expect to have a lucrative media career, no matter how true it might be. To keep your job, you have to pretend that the White Hate Nazi Klan Machine is still rolling along *Mississippi Burning*-style.

By the weekend, Cumia had deleted all tweets he'd ever made—everything, throughout his entire history on Twitter. In their stead, he then posted two pictures—one of them with a black friend of his named Carlton and the other with a white tranny who has admittedly amazing breasts. At some point over the weekend and apparently half-shitfaced, he posted a video of himself and Carlton singing a karaoke version of Paul McCartney and Stevie Wonder's treacly ode to interracial harmony, "Ebony and Ivory."

But these latest gestures seem snide, as if he's playing it for laughs. If so, good for him. Although he deleted all his tweets even after it was too late for him to keep his job, I have yet to hear the slightest evidence of him flat-out apologizing. For all I know—indeed, for all I *hope*—he may be sitting in a lawn chair, sipping a martini, and enjoying the sun in his backyard in Racistville, USA. If one day he winds up crying on camera and saying that he never meant what he said, I would prefer that you didn't tell me.

I've often thought that comedians are the last bastion of ballsiness in American media. That old plastic-surgery monster Joan Rivers called Barack Obama gay and Michelle Obama a "tranny," and I see no hint of her being forced to eat her words. Gilbert Gottfried, fired a few years ago from his gig as the voice of the Aflac duck because he made a joke on Twitter about Japanese tsunami victims, recently penned a brilliant *Playboy* essay bemoaning "The Apology Epidemic" that he says has destroyed modern comedy. If there is ever to be any significant cultural pushback against political correctness, a few gutsy popular comedians may represent the vanguard. But that's so foolishly hopeful, it's comical.

Anthony Cumia's critics—yea, they are legion, and they all seem to be fat white bearded males who wear glasses, voted for Obama, and collect *Star Wars* memorabilia—are quick to note that this isn't a "free speech" or a First Amendment issue. Rather, it's that ultra-rare occasion where the "free market" does something they like—namely, it strips ideological heretics of the ability to put food on the table. I'd be willing to accept their "free market" argument if they were open to the idea of a *true* free market—say, one in which employers were free *not* to hire loudmouthed urban black women for fear that they might call you a "white motherfucker" and repeatedly punch you if you don't ask them for permission before taking their picture. If we can all agree to that, then let freedom ring!

34

Wigger, Pleeze!

Sipping my iced coffee outside a café one Thursday night in Decatur, GA—a town with such a thriving lesbian ghetto that local wiseacres call it Dick Hater, GA—the stars magically aligned and I found myself seated next to a table of three fat white women huddled worshipfully around one fat black woman.

The fat white women all stared with adoration at the fat black woman. It seemed as if merely by being black, she was their guru. They laughed at everything she said—loudly. Clearly they enjoyed her salty, authentic vocal inflections and her sassy, mama-don't-take-no-mess attitude. When they weren't laughing at her jokes, they spoke somberly of justice and inclusivity and passion. I swear on a stack of Torahs that they also stressed the need for people to properly distinguish between inclusivity and passion, although I doubt that even *they* had a clue what the fuck they were talking about with that one.

But what rang clear as a copper bell on a crisp Alpine morning was that these three fat white presumed lesbians worshiped the fat black presumed lesbian merely because she was black and thus wasn't saddled with the historical guilt that emotionally cripples fat white lesbian women in the throes of a midlife racial identity crisis.

If they were only able to crawl inside this black woman's skin, they would do it. In fact, I suspect that's exactly what they did later that night.

As our society is currently constructed—or, rather, as our culture is currently dictated to us—there is no emotional satisfaction in being white. There is only pain and guilt and apologies. And this is why so many whites seek refuge in pretending to be black. They talk black, think black, and even try to look black. Some even claim that they're black.

Earlier that day before I encountered the interracial fat lesbian social-justice quartet at the Dick Hater coffee shop, Taki's Mag writer (and accused Judeophile) Kathy Shaidle informed me of the odd case of one Rachel Dolezal, the NAACP Branch President of Spokane, WA who for years has successfully "passed" as a black woman but was recently outed as a natural-born blue-eyed devil.

She wasn't pretending to be black in order to experience their suffering. She was pretending to be black so she could reap the benefits. This wasn't *Black Like Me*. It was *Black Like She*.

In a video that went viral in 2015, a reporter corners Dolezal about her claims that her dad was black. Behind blue eyes, Dolezal affirms that yes, indeed, sure, yup, her dad was black, yes, yeah, mm-hmm, he was. But when the reporter presses the subject, she walks away.

For years Dolezal has claimed her dad was coal-black and that she's given birth to black sons. But then her white parents revealed that she's almost entirely of European descent, with the only other tincture being perhaps a gentle sprinkling of "Native American." Then one of her alleged "sons" revealed that he was merely her black stepbrother and that she often urged him to lie to others that she was black. It seemed as if her parents and her black step-bro all wished for the nutty charade to end.

In addition to birthing Rachel, her parents also adopted four black children. Like their natural-born daughter, they apparently loved basking in the whole black experience, too. But despite their wide-eyed progressive earnestness—or perhaps as collateral damage from it—they say their daughter started acting increasingly hostile toward them around 2006 or 2007. As luck would have it, this was also when Rachel began her attempt to visually "transition" into blackness. She seems to have already felt she was there internally—she merely needed a new coat of paint to finish the renovation job.

Miz Rachel is either baking her naturally melanin-deficient skin orange at a tanning salon or applying bronze-colored makeup in an act of theatrical deception that is only different from full-blown minstrel-show blackface in terms of hue.

The term "wigger" is a portmanteau of "white" and a word beginning in "n" that is so horrible, I just literally shrieked out loud at the mere thought of typing it.

But Rachel Dolezal—who was born with blonde hair, blue eyes, and pale white skin—appears to also be a *literal* wigger, assuming that is indeed a kinky-haired black-woman's wig she was wearing in that video. If not, she must pay her stylist bookoo bucks to blackify her God-given Nordic mane. In a video where she bemoans the proliferation of wealthy white males on US currency, she's rockin' some blond cornrows that I strongly suspect are hair extensions.

She was sportin' similar golden cornrows in pictures taken with a black male Mississippi rap artist who was briefly her fiancé a couple years ago. If you have the stomach for such things, that link contains a music video he dedicated to Rachel containing the following lyrics:

> *Your legs are the sensual bridges to heaven...*
> *The sweetest vajayjay more cosmic than the Milky Way.*

Dolezal eventually broke off the engagement with that addled sap, but she did marry a black man back in Mississippi in 2000. Wedding pictures reveal that Dolezal had yet to begin her visual transition toward blackness and was, at least to the naked eye, still a chubby, blonde-haired white girl. She and her Token Black Husband divorced four years later. But—much as my presumed white lesbians at the coffee shop—she appears to have developed a taste for the dark meat.

Over the years, Dolezal also claimed to have been victimized repeatedly by hate crimes. Police were unable to verify a single allegation of hers. After it was revealed that Spokane's black NAACP leader was a lyin'-ass honky bitch, they closed their investigations into her hate-crime complaints.

Faced with yet another large-scale embarrassment, prog pundits were quick to explain that a white woman claiming she's black is an insult to black people. They tried arguing...somehow...that even though race doesn't exist, white people are not permitted to pretend that they're black people.

Mind you, these are precisely the same people who celebrated Bruce Jenner's recent "transition" into a thing called "Caitlyn." But they were unflinching in the assertion that although "transgender" is real and should be celebrated, "transracial" is fantasy and should be condemned.

I'll let you kids all work it out amongst yourselves. But seriously, thanks for all the laughs. You guys are hilarious.

35

Race Is a Social Construct, So I'm a Poor Black Orphan

If you're generally a busy bumblebee like I am, you don't have time to sit around all day socially constructing things. Thus, I am *so* glad that there are volunteers who do this work for me—and at no charge, to boot! Merely keeping up with the latest culturally acceptable semantic terms is a full-time job in itself, and I am truly grateful there are people out there who tell me what to say and how to think. I am also in awe of their ability to make shit up while believing it's true. Hats off to them—and I say that as a man who owns about twenty hats.

So for those of you who are far more socially conscious than I am, please be patient with me, because I'm just trying to keep up here—at least as I've been led to understand it, according to the latest science from The Global Science Foundation or whatever it's called—homosexuality is genetically hardwired, but race and gender are only *ideas*, right? Is that the latest science? Got it. Bookmarked and filed. I will pick that, lick that, stick that, and flick that.

In other words, gay people can't help it. That explains a lot.

But I'm so glad that science has proved that gender and race are simply dumb myths concocted by capitalist robber barons to keep us all angry at one another rather than working together to raise the minimum wage at Burger King.

These last few years have been a glitter-spackled, fuchsia-tinted explosion of progress as the mighty transgendered have finally received respect and official protection in society now that we all realize that they are actually—scientifically and medically and socially and *everything*—women living in men's bodies rather than sad and maladjusted delusional crazy people who are hacking themselves to pieces while chasing a dream. I am SO glad that's out of the way.

But as always, my allies and comrades and fellow travelers, there is more work for us to do. I know that it seems like there's *always* more work for us to do, but if we didn't have that work, then we wouldn't be "us," now, would we? And it's not as if any of us are working, anyway.

We've made tremendous progress with destroying, defaming, and defiling the very notion of gender. For that, I give you two thumbs up. But we have a long, long, LONG way to go when it comes to race. Since we've successfully swung our unforgiving ball-peen hammers at the false idea that gender is real, let's swing 'em around at the eternal fiction that is "race." As everyone who's, like, read a book knows, "race" a really bad and harmful idea that you should mentally electroshock out of your head the moment it dares to creep inside your skull.

Race is only an idea. It doesn't exist in the real world. So if you get the idea that you belong to another race, you should run with that idea. Even if you're obviously more ginger than a frosty bottle of ginger ale, you can be as black or brown or red or yellow as you want. It's objectively no more true or false than the idea that you're "white," even though that's what black people at the subway station are always calling you late at night when they're surrounding you and asking for money. They may seem a little gruff to you, but you don't realize that they are only showing you the hate that hate created, so it's not really hate at all—it's more like revolutionary love.

WHITENESS: THE ORIGINAL SIN   239

But if race and gender are mere social constructs, and since we as a society already celebrate the fact that you can be whatever gender you wish to be, the same should apply for your "race." As they say, what's good for the goose is good for the gender.

So to all the transgendered out there—and believe me, I celebrate you, I do—please scooch over and make a little room on your Rainbow Bus for the "transracial," AKA the "transethnic." I'm talking about a totally different phenomenon here—in the same way that trannies...sorry, *transsexuals*...sorry, *the transgendered*—believe they are women in men's bodies, the transracial and transethnic identify with a race and/or culture other than their own.

And who could argue? If gender is only a malleable, elastic, easily reshaped and redefined idea, shouldn't the same concept apply to race? If someone can truly change their gender, why can't they switch races, too?

DNA is an oppressively hierarchal social construct at least as harmful as the delusion that estrogen has anything to do with female behavior. That whole rotten "DNA" sham was constructed by some old white racist named James Watson. It's about as reliable as astrology.

My DNA test says I am 100% European, nearly all of it Northern European. However, this doesn't mean that I enjoy lutefisk and scented candles. Therefore, these tests are highly unscientific.

Since race is merely an idea—a pinch of invisible magical dust held lightly between the thumb and forefinger—I can close my eyes, wiggle my nose, click my heels, and reconstruct myself as a black man of pure dark-chocolate 100% swampy sub-Saharan ancestry, and I don't care if you like it or not. No, actually, I *do* care if you like it—in other words, I will MAKE you like it. And since none of you will be able to find my black parents, I will also register as an orphan, depending on whether I qualify for government assistance based on that status. I would think that being a poor black orphan would be worth—what?—at least $500 combined monthly from local agencies and President Obama's personal stash? I can be whatever I want to be, and you can't stop me, and that's my right, and I'll take it all the way to the Supreme Court, so don't push me, or I will call you a hater and get you fired from your job.

We live in a new world where technology enables you to be anyone you can afford to be. If I can get my health insurance to cover it, I will gladly keep switching races so long as it helps me work my hustle. I will choose to be whatever race is most socially and financially advantageous for me at any given time. Even if I have to be a Filipino, I suppose I could handle it. Armenian would be really pushing it. But otherwise, I'm cool. And no Asian. Or Mexican.

On second thought, I'll just stay white.

36

Thor Losers

A single week in July 2014 was a trifecta for Cultural Marxism in the comic-book world: Archie Andrews was shot to death trying to protect a gay senator, Captain America became black, and the Mighty Thor had a sex change.

Archie Andrews, the freckle-faced, milkshake-drinking ginger who has epitomized American wholesomeness since 1941, was murdered in *Life With Archie* #36. His friend Kevin Keller, an openly gay white senator with a black husband, was campaigning for gun control and was being threatened by some stereotypically rendered right-wing gun nut. But Archie stepped in and "heroically" ate a bullet for him.

"Archie is not a superhero like all the rest of the comic book characters," explained Jon Goldwater, co-CEO of Archie Comics. "He's human. He's a person. When you wound him, he bleeds. He knows that. If anything, I think his death is more impactful because of that." (The company's other co-CEO is Nancy Silberkleit, who has been sued for sexual harassment by reportedly referring to all male employees as "Penis" rather than their names. She denied such harassment was even possible since males are not a "protected class." At press time, I could not verify whether she also uses tremendously annoying words such as "impactful.")

I'll bet you didn't know that before he gave his life to save a gay senator, Archie also spawned an interracial baby with a black woman.

Marvel Comics announced that the role of Captain America—who, like Archie, has existed as a Caucasian since 1941—will be assumed by a black man from Harlem who until now has played a sidekick known as "The Falcon." The original Captain America the white one—is giving his role over to The Falcon because he is now 90 years old and too feeble to be a superhero anymore.

"In 2014, this should be a thing that we shrug off," says Marvel executive editor Tom Brevoort about the new black Captain America. "It shouldn't be seen as revolutionary, but it still feels exciting."

So if it's no big thing, why did you do it in the first place, and why does it feel "exciting" to you?

Marvel also announced that the Mighty Thor, who has existed as a muscular male thunder god in Nordic folklore for millennia and became a male comic-book hero in 1962, will transmogrify into a woman starting in October 2014, since the male Thor has been deemed "unworthy" to wield his legendary hammer. "This is not She-Thor," said series writer Jason Aaron. "This is not Lady Thor. This is not Thorita. This is THOR. This is the THOR of the Marvel Universe. But it's unlike any Thor we've ever seen before."

In Norse mythology, Thor has a golden-haired wife named Sif. They could have easily made her into a comic-book superhero and thus avoided meddling with ancient European cultural tradition. The fact that they didn't suggests that the primary motive is meddling with ancient European cultural tradition.

But these three cases are hardly the first instances of PC injecting itself virus-like into the comic-book world in an attempt to mold impressionable young minds.

In 2011, Marvel murdered the Caucasian Peter Parker and swapped him out for the half-black/half-Puerto Rican "Miles Morales" as the human being who lurks beneath Spider-Man's mask. According to Marvel's half-Mexican Editor in Chief Alex Alonso, his writers' "job is to re-imagine characters in a forward-thinking, progressive manner....As a Hispanic, it is nice to see Spider-Man's...last name resemble the last name of my son."

Also in 2011, Action Comics had Superman—whose motto had been "truth, justice, and the American way"—appear before the United Nations to renounce his American citizenship because he'd become disgusted with the American way.

Batwoman, originally conceived in 1956 as a presumably heterosexual *shiksa*, reemerged in 2006 as a Jewish lesbian.

Nick Fury had existed as a Marvel Comics superhero since 1956 as a one-eyed white man. He's still chugging along, but in 2001 he was one-upped by Ultimate Nick Fury, a one-eyed black man.

In 2012, DC Comics' Green Lantern came out of the closet as a homosexual and married another man.

The year 2013 saw the unveiling of Ms. Marvel, apparently the world's first Pakistani Muslim comic-book superheroine.

And the modern X-Men represent a whole cast of "mutants" that include a Holocaust survivor, a Malcolm X clone, and a full *dozen* gay and bisexual superheroes.

When modern white singers such as Miley Cyrus twerk with black backup dancers and Katy Perry wears a geisha costume, the leftist chorus howls that they are guilty of the sin of "cultural appropriation," and we all know that such appropriation isn't appropriate.

Why, then, don't we hear the same cries of "cultural appropriation" when Archie Comics' Jewish co-CEOs green-light Archie's murder in defense of a gay senator or Marvel's Hispanic editor decides to make Captain America black and Thor into a woman? Why, especially, is a non-Nordic male allowed to rub his grubby fingers all over an ancient Nordic male god to suit his half-assed "progressive" agenda?

Would Nancy Silberkleit be OK with a film version where a Nazi skinhead plays the role of Moses? Would Alex Alonso be just *bueno* if Larry the Cable Guy were to portray Che Guevara in a cable-TV movie? Of course they wouldn't. They don't think it's "progressive" for anyone to mess with *their* cultural icons.

What they're doing goes far beyond mere "cultural appropriation." This is cultural pillaging.

37

First They Came for the Albinos

Is there a man among us willing to shed a tear for the poor persecuted albinos of modern East Africa?

No?

Tough crowd.

OK, how about if I were to sketch out a convoluted and highly dubious scenario in which African albinos were the ancient progenitors of modern Caucasians, that they were driven into Europe tens of thousands of years ago as a result of racist persecution from black Africans, and that any resultant pillaging and plundering of Africa by white Europeans can then be justified as payback against our original oppressors?

It's unlikely, but it's fun to pretend it's plausible. It's fun in the same way that the Solutrean hypothesis is fun—whether or not it's true, even attempting to argue that the "original" Americans were European rather than Asian subverts the whole Guilt Narrative in a way that confounds, flusters, and befuddles those misguided losers who are always seeking repentance and reparations.

By the same token, arguing that white-skinned Africans were the first large-scale victims of racial persecution in the world—that the original great human exodus from Africa was less a peaceful migration than it was a violent purge of light-skinned undesirables, that it was less "out of Africa" and more "get the hell out of Africa"—gives white people a moral leg up in the stubbornly idiotic game of racial karma and intergenerational guilt-tripping.

In February 2015, Tanzanian police reported that they found the hacked-up body of a year-old male albino. His missing body parts are presumed to have been funneled into a highly lucrative black-magic market where a single albino body can fetch up to $75,000. You see, many Africans—including those well-heeled enough to cough up $75K just for a dead albino—believe that even though albinos themselves are cursed, their body parts can work magical wonders and bring great health, prosperity, success, popularity, sex appeal, and all of the other things that dumb primitive minds who believe in magic always seem to lack.

Estimates vary, but since the year 2000 anywhere from 70-200 albinos have been mercilessly hunted "like animals" and hacked to death in East Africa to fuel this odd and gruesome corpse-grinding market demand. Victims often have their limbs severed while they're alive due to a superstition that their dead body parts will glow with added mojo if the victim was screaming while they were being slaughtered.

In Zimbabwe, HIV-afflicted men will often rape albino women based on the superstition that it will cure them of their incurable disease.

Far be it from me to ever suggest that such a chokingly thick climate of prehistoric superstition may in some way be related to many of the travails and indignities that persist to this very day in modern Africa. As previously implied, my intention here—however insincere—is not to malign black Africans but instead to instill a sense of kinship, however fraudulent, between white people and albino Africans.

Phenotypically, the most easily targeted "cultural other" on the planet may be the hapless albino stranded somewhere in the malarial backwaters of sub-Saharan Africa. Folkloric traditions teach that albinos are ghosts and therefore less than human. They are "treated like lepers" and routinely pushed to society's fringes. "Over time, the frustration is so much that it affects you negatively," one female Zimbabwean albino with an unpronounceable name laments. "If you keep on thinking about what people say about you or do to you, you will have tears on your cheeks forever."

In a way—and this is rare with me—I can empathize. I've always felt sorry for albinos mainly because they're so goddamned *weird*-looking that I can't imagine life is easy for them. And I must seize this opportunity to announce that at various times in my life I have owned records by the white albino Edgar Winter and the black albino Yellowman, so it cannot be said that I've ever personally discriminated against an albino, at least not to my recollection—or at least, as memory serves, not when anyone was watching.

I claim no expertise in human migratory patterns over the past 100,000 years or so, which is why I elect to rely entirely on crudely designed black-nationalist websites that argue modern Caucasians are the direct descendants of African albinos. At least that way, no one can accuse me of being a racist.

According to a site that calls itself "Real History":

> *All the data and "Common Sense" clearly shows that White Europeans are the "Fixed" Albinos of the original Black Indians (Dravidians) of India, who moved further north to Central Asia, seeking solace and less Sunlight. They are primarily of the OCA-2 type Albinism, indicated by Blonde Hair, Blue Eyes, Pale – but not White Skin, the ability to "Tan" and Normal Eyesight. But Albinism is a disease – A "Defect" if you will – and Europeans seem determined not to admit that.*

Ouch. He's good. No use denying it anymore—I am a diseased, defective descendant of outcast albinos. I am still more proficient at math than almost anyone south of the Sahara, but that doesn't make it OK.

A site called Stewart Synopsis explains the Great Albino Migration:

> *Eventually most of the "white skinned" off springs [sic] of "African" mothers and fathers formed several groups and began to migrate northward through Egypt to another area of Africa which is now called Europe, seeking a more hospitable living environment and to escape the intensity of the equatorial hot climate of the great river valleys and great lakes region of Central, Eastern and Southern Africa which was then and still is South of what is now called Egypt.*

All right then. Using unsubstantiated statements culled strictly from black-nationalist websites, I have established that what are currently known as so-called "white people" are actually genetically defective refugee African albinos who were persecuted by black Africans in ancient times. I have also established that African albinos continue to be persecuted to this day, as their tormentors blithely string the African countryside with the mutilated torsos of albino toddlers who screamed loudly as they were being killed. In this lethal game of tag, I have tagged black Africans as the historical inventors of skin-based racism, discrimination, and violent hate crimes. And as soon as I can find a good Jewish lawyer, I'm going to sue the pants off them, assuming that people wear pants in Africa.

38

In Defense of Neanderthals

The most stubbornly hypocritical glitch in the egalitarian mindset is that eugenics is roundly and vigorously dismissed as a dangerous and discredited pseudoscience...*unless* it can be wielded to portray ideological enemies as genetically inferior throwbacks.

Thus, the same sheltered, daydreaming buttercups that strain to deny even basic visual differences between ethnic groups are the first to blame rural white poverty on things such as inbreeding and overall crappy genes. In such cases, eugenics are not only suddenly real, they are highly pertinent—decisive, even.

The same double standard permits politicians—who'd never dare publicly suggest that sub-Saharan Africa is not exactly the Hope Diamond of intellectual achievement—to smear large swaths of people who don't kowtow to their dim notions of "progress" as "Neanderthals."

Vice President Joseph Biden, that asshole, recently referred to Republicans as "Neanderthals." A couple of years ago, current Secretary of State John Kerry, who resembles an archeological dig even while alive, dismissed global-warming critics as "Neanderthals." In 2003, now-dead Senator Ted Kennedy said he would resist the appointment of any "Neanderthal" that George W. Bush might nominate as a judge. The Daily Kos, that festering armpit of self-congratulatory leftist delusion, recently suggested that NRA members possessed the "Neanderthal gene."

The pejorative "Neanderthal," despite being anthropologically hurtful and unabashedly *Homo sapiens*-supremacist, is thrown around with gleeful impunity by the selfsame egalitards who insist that everyone is created equal...except, of course, for the knuckle-dragging prehistoric losers who don't think like they do.

If I know one thing about people, it's that they need to feel superior to other people, and since it's no longer culturally permissible to suggest that sub-Saharan Africa may be a teeny bit backward, one is free to indulge their innate craving to feel superior at the expense of the stocky, hairy, big-browed, club-wielding descendants of *Homo neanderthalen-sis* whose genetic vestiges now listen to heavy metal, attend NASCAR races, own hunting rifles, pray to Jesus, handle serpents, and vote Republican.

Hell, it's possible that the word "Neanderthal"—or at least a grunted prehistoric synonym for it—was the original racial slur.

In its pejorative usage amid the modern Anglosphere, "Neanderthal" is exclusively used to demean whites. In fairness, pale skin, blue eyes, and red hair were all Neanderthal traits. But although being Neanderthal *is* a white thing, it is not exclusively so. A landmark 2010 study suggested that not only did ancient Neanderthals breed with modern humans, all modern groups *except* for sub-Saharan Africans possess a small percentage of Neanderthal DNA.

So genetically, humans can somewhat tidily be divided into two groups: those who have Neanderthal DNA...and black people. If a black person's DNA test reveals any Neanderthal ancestry, you can assume they have some cream in their coffee.

But Ted Kennedy? John Kerry? Joe Biden, that asshole? Neanderthals, every last one of them. And *self-hating* Neanderthals at that. The worst kind.

The percentage of Neanderthal DNA among the world's six billion or so nonblacks usually ranges from 1-4%; a recent DNA test suggested that my own quotient is 3%, meaning I'm slightly more Neanderthal than the average European and WAAYYYYYY more Neanderthal than Mike Tyson, MC Hammer, and Kim Fields, that nice black girl who played Tootie on *The Facts of Life*.

When the 2010 DNA study was published, white-hating hominids gleefully announced that only "African peoples are 100 percent human," that Europeans' lingering Neanderthal DNA formed "the prehistoric sources of the white race's aggression, racism and sexism," that ""white people are descended from unwashed hairy beasts not our African brethren," and that "Africans are true *Homo sapiens*, while the rest are watered down Neanderthal inbreds."

That's all very cute, except for the fact that the places where people are "100 percent human" tend to fall far behind the cavemen's ancestral homelands when it comes to trifles such as longevity, technology, written languages, and living standards.

It's touchy and toxic to ponder how those dumbass troglodytes were able to build civilizations that remain advanced far beyond those of the pure humans. Though we've all been trained to equate "Neanderthal" with "stupid," it's generally

accepted that Neanderthal brains were at least as
large as those of *Homo sapiens*, but people will start
calling you bad names if you dare raise the topic
of differences in brain size among human groups.
Therefore, the more plausible explanation for why
primitive subhumans consistently outperform fully
evolved humans is because they use the subtly per-
suasive methods of tricknology.

Neanderthals weren't quite as dimwitted as, say,
Barney Rubble or the giant dumb caveman in
Eegah. They were a humble and hardworking folk
who built homes and fashioned tools. They buried
their dead, sometimes with flowers. They had a
"sense of compassion" that led them to care for disabled children and the elderly. According to one
website, they "lived in family groups, had names,
hunted game, usually at night in groups, baked
acorn meal bread, and had language, religion, cuisine, medicine, trade, tools, crafts and art, including
music, dance and body paint."

I can get behind all of that except for the body
painting.

One could view the first dusky, lanky *Homo sapiens*
who ventured north from southern Africa's steamy
jungles and into the Middle East, Europe, and Asia
as *immigrants*. Or one could view them as *colonists*.
One could even view them as *biological predators*

who almost completely eliminated the indigenous population. This is a case where the historical record is by necessity prehistoric, so it remains unclear why the appearance of interlopers out of Africa coincided somewhat with the gradual extinction of a Neanderthal population that had resided in Europe for nearly half a million years. Maybe it was all a wacky coincidence. Or maybe it was the first large-scale genocide in human history.

Still, those kooky cavemen are largely gone, and I'd like to place at least *some* of the blame on Africans because, well, *that's what I do.* But they are not entirely gone. Strains of their ancient blood course through my veins, causing that sudden involuntary Berserker thrill whenever I accidentally hear a Led Zeppelin song.

But dead or alive, I believe it's time Neanderthals received their due respect, or, as the so-called "pure humans" like to say, their "props." So to all you pure, fully evolved humans out there who flit breezily through this world unencumbered with even a wisp of Neanderthal DNA: I want you to know that although we may not look and act like it, *we* are human, too, and we demand that you respect that part, goddamnit! We are your sons, your daughters, your brothers, and your sisters. When you cut a Neanderthal, does he not bleed? Huh? Does he not? Even if he's a "she"? Of course she does! So before we all start stabbing one another, we should agree that we all bleed.

To all my fellow cavemen, cavewomen, and cavechildren: How much longer will we endure their insults? How much longer must we suffer the slings and arrows of their arrogant evolutionary disdain? "No longer," I say. Those "Geico Caveman" commercials were a good start, but we need more positive depictions of Neanderthals throughout popular culture. No more anti-Neanderthal slurs and no more anti-Neanderthal job discrimination. Working together we were able to kick a woolly mammoth's ass, so these modern humans don't stand a chance against us. Do not give up hope. Burn bright, little Neanderthal flame. There's a light at the end of the cave.

39

Of Heritage and Hate

Stone Mountain is a 1,700-foot-tall grey dome rock located about a half-hour due east of downtown Atlanta. On its northern face is the world's largest bas-relief carving—bigger even than the carving at Mouth Rushmore. It depicts Confederate heroes Robert E. Lee, Stonewall Jackson, and Jefferson Davis. The mountain also features a Confederate battle flag at the base of its hiking trail.

Stone Mountain is also where the Ku Klux Klan reinvented itself in 1915 under the direction of William J. Simmons. As legend has it, the Klan would conduct nighttime cross burnings from atop that massive rock to frighten the Atlanta area's entire black population in one big theatrical stroke of political terror.

Fast-forward a hundred years, and the Klan has clearly lost. The surrounding town of Stone Mountain is now over 75% black and about 16% white. And Atlanta hasn't had a white mayor since the early 1970s.

June 2015's Charleston church shooting—involving a killer who had sullenly posed for selfies hoisting a small Rebel flag—was used as an excuse to launch a full-on cultural purge of all Confederate symbols by those who hate what they insist those symbols represent. And they insist those symbols represent HATE. And they *hate* that. Those symbols represent intolerance. And they *will not tolerate* that.

Stone Mountain might as well be the Confederate Matterhorn. It is a huge—quite literally the largest—target for the fanatics who are seeking to forever expunge all remotely respectful memorials to Confederate and Southern white history.

Recently a spokesman for Atlanta's NAACP demanded that the Confederate carving "be sandblasted off" Stone Mountain's side. He also urged authorities to remove the Rebel flag from the mountain's base.

This raised the hackles and chafed the sunburned necks of Confederate sympathizers across Georgia. Insisting that the flag represented "heritage, not hate," they arranged for a pro-Confederate rally one Saturday morning in July 2015 at Stone Mountain Park.

I couldn't resist attending. I lived in the city of Stone Mountain for nearly four years and have also scaled that giant grey slab dozens of times. I met some real oddballs climbing up that hiking trail—such as the guy who allegedly popularized the term "Black Power."

In a Facebook post that has since been deleted, the rally's organizers stressed that any overt displays of "hate" would not be tolerated:

1.) NO racial slurs or offensive remarks

2.) NO alcohol, we do know its [sic] illegal and that will be opportunity for tickets/arrests

3.) NO taunting other vehicles, flipping other people off during the ride

4.) NO burning any flags of any type regardless of which flag

5.) STAY peaceful, which means NO violence....
Possibly media and cameras, ONE piece of negativity and that will be what goes Viral and that is what we will be remembered for. This is to show our support BC we care about where we live and grew up, lets [sic] keep this Clean and Peaceful!

The event took place two days after a rather fishy "hate crime" involving the placement of Rebel flags on the lawn outside MLK's hallowed Ebenezer Baptist Church.

I arrived at the park around 11AM on Saturday, and I'd never seen the place deader, even on weekdays. I figured that the rally would be held at the foot of the Confederate carving, but when I got there I saw only a smattering of mostly foreign-looking tourists placidly grazing about.

A traffic cop redirected me to the rally's location—a remote parking lot designed to handle overflow from the main parking lot. In my dozens of trips to this park, I'd never even been aware of this parking lot's existence.

And there suddenly, like cultural porno, I saw it—a sea of Rebel flags flapping in the hot and muggy haze. I'd estimate the crowd at between 300 and 400, and good Lord, were they a torn-up, chewed-up, rough-hewn, beaten-down—yet proud—bunch. They wore their history—in particular, their intergenerational defeat and ongoing public humiliation—on their faces. Fuck those absurdly wealthy and culturally hostile scalawags at the Southern Poverty Law Center—here was the *true* Southern poverty, the generations of want and suffering and being scapegoated and trying to scratch out an existence in a conquered land where their conquerors seek to scratch *them* out of existence.

One hundred and fifty years after the Civil War ended, here was a perpetually maligned demographic that had witnessed almost everything, including their dignity, being stripped from them.

And now the professional carpetbagger class was trying to take away that flag, which is all that many of them have left. And for all the pious homilies being uttered about how that flag represented "hate," these pontificators never bother to hide their sneering, fuming hatred for these poor unwashed white Southern proles.

The section of the parking lot hosting the "event" was fenced in, which seemed appropriate—this was a temporary animal shelter for the stray dogs of the Lost Cause. It was a clumsy setup, with the focus of the festivities the flatbed of a pickup truck rigged with a static-laden sound system. To help keep the peace, camouflage-clad members of the Georgia Militia roamed the premises carrying rifles.

I milled around taking pictures and stopping to eavesdrop whenever it sounded like an argument was erupting. Some earnest young black dudes were trying to explain to a bearded peckerwood that the Rebel flag represented pain for black people, but the peckerwood said it represented family and history and Southern soil.

Then suddenly the crowd started chanting, "KKK! Go away!" They surrounded a white-bearded man toting a Rebel flag but who had a small Klan insignia patch stitched to the front of his bucket hat. They shouted him right out of the parking lot. "Fuck the KKK. Fuck that shit. Get that asshole out of here."

Strange crowd, this one. They were taking this "heritage, not hate" thing literally.

Apart from the lone-wolf Klansman, the only other troublemakers were small pockets of white and black progressives who showed up to taunt the crowd. Never mind that this is roughly as rude as the Westboro Baptist Church showing up to taunt fallen war heroes. There was a group from the Revolutionary Communist Party standing right outside the fence protesting victims of police brutality but failing to explain what any of this had to do with the Rebel flag.

Then there was a bearded white radical who burned and stomped on a Rebel flag right outside of the fence. This led to much mutual screaming and taunting until most of the attendees were convinced it was best to ignore this hairy agitator. But if you could actually quantify hatred, I'd bet this bearded radical had much more of it coursing through his bloodstream than anyone around him.

And then, finally, came what the party-crashers were looking for. A genetically challenged-looking ginger male in a pink baseball cap called a black girl a "greasy monkey nigger bitch." The black girl in question, who was wearing a shirt celebrating her "blackness," began howling and screaming and clawing and swinging like a Jerry Springer guest before cops were able to restore order. Her friend, a portly black woman with a giant black leather earring in the shape of Mother Africa, shouted at someone in the crowd, "What if I called you a greasy inbred stringy-haired cracker?"

"I'd be offended," they replied.

"But 'cracker' isn't offensive!" she insisted.

"Shouldn't that be for the crackers to decide?" I asked her. She either didn't hear me or she didn't want to answer the question. Maybe she simply assumed it was for her to decide what was offensive and what wasn't.

To my immense delight—seriously, it was like a teenage girl learning that Justin Bieber had suddenly shown up—I was informed that the tall black dude in sunglasses and checkered bucket hat was Georgia Congressman Hank Johnson, infamous for publicly wondering whether Guam would capsize if the US were to send too many Marines to the island. I have been brutally unkind to Johnson in the past. In fact, the only time I'd voted in the previous ten years was in a local election for whomever was running against Hank Johnson, because I thought it was criminal that a man of his meager intellect should be in the US Congress.

Everyone at the event who was aware of Johnson's presence—as well as all of my friends after being informed of it—made the same joke about whether Johnson was worried if the parking lot might capsize.

But Johnson had recently told the press he didn't have a problem with the flags at Stone Mountain because they represented history. He only objected to Confederate flags flying over government buildings. He reiterated this point to me. He even rolled his eyes when I mentioned the NAACP's suggestion that the Confederate carving should be sandblasted from the side of the mountain. "Nah, c'mon, man—that's history. It's history. Leave it alone."

It was a refreshing and unexpectedly hilarious burst of common sense from the unlikeliest suspect in Georgia. Hank Johnson actually agreed with the rally-goers—this was about heritage, not hate. I posed for a photo with him before moving on into the crowd again.

Yet another young black male was pleading with attendees about how he felt the flag was a provocation, and the attendees kept insisting it had nothing to do with him, especially not with hating him. But he told them that it did. And they kept insisting that it didn't.

Smirking at an argument that kept going in circles, one peckerwood quipped to me, "That's one of those deals where ain't nobody going to get ahead."

And that pithy quote encapsulated the entire event. It was an argument over what *symbols* represent—an argument that no one could ever win, because there is no objective answer. In the end, symbols represent whatever someone wants them to represent. One person's heritage is another person's hate. And the twain shall never agree.

40

Brett Kavanaugh Is a White Man

In case you've been vacationing on Pluto and were unaware, during his confirmation process Supreme Court nominee Brett Kavanaugh was being accused of tryin' ta sorta do somethin'-somethin' to a woman in the early 1980s when he was 17 and she was 15.

Did he do it? Don't know. Wasn't there.

Personally, I have no pit bull in this Rape Game. His guilt or innocence should have been determined way back in the early 1980s by a court of law, but his alleged victim is a patient woman who decided to wait about three and a half decades before saying anything publicly.

Both Kavanaugh and his accuser, a weepy, lumpy-faced gal named Christina Blasey Ford, are white. You would notice that immediately upon seeing them. But although the accuser and accused are both white, I don't see any evidence of either one of them making a point of it.

Beyond that, I don't see how it's relevant. As we all know, people of all colors can rape and get raped. That's part of the core meaning of equality. In times of war, the winning side tends to rape the losing side's women. In many cases, war is based upon ethnic divisions. But since both parties here are white, it's hard to see race as a motivating factor in whether or not he aggressively tugged at her panties lo, all those years ago.

Don't try telling that to our cultural experts in the media. Judging from their leap to judgment, Brett Kavanaugh is a white male rapist who rapes because white men are rapists who feel it's their God-given right to rape, and their God is white in case you were wondering.

If you think I'm overstating things, choke on this thick, veiny text block:

> Hell hath no fury like a white man told he can't take whatever he wants whenever he wants it.
> —Reporter Steven W. Thrasher

Kavanaugh reeks of white entitlement.
—*Black activist Touré*

Kavanaugh is the kind of dangerous, entitled white man many of us have encountered all throughout our lives. If he is confirmed, I'm even more afraid of the revenge he'll seek after this hearing.
—*Activist Raquel Willis*

Time to utterly crush the old white boy power base in Washington. Because it looks like this committee and it looks like Biff Kavanaugh and it needs to be eviscerated permanently...it is the old America and must give way to the new and only version worthy of its promise
—*Pathologically anti-white race-baiter Tim Wise*

Kavanaugh feels betrayed because he's a born-into-privilege white man who got to his station in life by sucking up and shitting down.
—*Reporter Tina Dupuy*

Arrogant white men must have no place...Women's views, women's pain, and the struggles of anyone other than the patrician white male, simply do not count when a senior white male's reputation or future is at stake....It is time they are put out to pasture....The arrogant white male has no place in making the laws of this wonderful country.
—*Letter to the Durango Herald*

Oh boy—Kavanaugh is going full angry belittled margin-alized white man. Tough sell for today
—Reporter Luke Russert

They know the optics of 11 white men questioning Dr. Ford ... will be so harmful and so damaging to the GOP.
—CNN Analyst Areva Martin

What are those — that collection of old white men going to do?
—MSNBC analyst Cynthia Alksne

Unfuckingbelievable. Ford was entitled to rage but held back. Instead Kavanaugh rages, an entitled white man who cannot abide being challenged.
—Author Rabia O'Chaudry

The angry white man – crying routine is so typical of an alcoholic. Is #Kavanaugh drunk?
—Author Eva Golinger

The Republicans, it happens to be 11 white men still on that side....The Republicans, it is 11 white men, talk to me about how you think the tone inside this hearing on Monday will be perceived....On the Republican side, all 11 are white men.
— CNN host John Berman

The Republican side on the Senate Judiciary Committee is all white men....

— *Irin Carmon, senior correspondent for New York Magazine, on MSNBC*

Once again, it will be all white men on the Republican side of the Judiciary Committee questioning both Judge Kavanaugh and Doctor Ford.
—*CNN anchor Poppy Harlow*

It is a lineup of white guys over the age of 50.
—*MSNBC anchor Stephanie Ruhle*

Are these Republican white men essentially going to ask her if she's telling the truth? Are they going to question her credibility?
—*MSNBC guest and former Hillary Clinton campaign official Adrienne Elrod*

Women across this nation should be outraged at what these white men senators are doing to this woman.
—*Rep. John Garamendi, D-California*

These white men, old by the way, are not protecting women. They're protecting a man who is probably guilty.
—*Joy Behar*

Republican Party = white male party. They don't care about women and they don't care about the future. They care about the past where all white men are in power. Rape is fine. Keep minorities and women down. All white men, oh, and Ben Carson
—*Chelsea Handler*

Court Pick Steals a Page From Trump's Playbook on White Male Anger
—*WRAL.com*

The answer is plain: Conservative voices want to give Kavanaugh a pass because he is a white man who will represent their interests....We must call out the demons of white privilege that allow white men to be considered innocent from the very start while ethnic groups such as blacks in this country go on trial even after their own blood has unjustly been spilled.
—*Religion News*

Of course, you know that they'll be fine, that this is a bump in the road, that when privileged white men fall, they somehow fall up as if gravity doesn't apply.
—*Damon Young, The Root*

call your senators and tell them to vote no for Kavanaugh – the future of our country deserves more than a privileged white boy who's Spent his whole life over-drinking and can't answer a simple question without acting more immature about it than a 4 year old.
—*Parkland shooting survivor Emma Gonzalez, AKA the "lesbian skinhead"*

Brett Kavanaugh and America's Insistence on White Male Virtue...To watch him weaponize his rage, his tears, and his silence throughout that dreadful hearing was to watch a white man used to acting with impunity. This

was white male arrogance on display. And it was a sight.
—Anne Branigin, The Root

But the histrionics of Graham and Kavanaugh showed once again how hell hath no fury like an entitled white man denied. No humility. No contrition. No humanity beyond his narrow interests.
—Jonathan Capehart, The Washington Post

This Was the Hour of White Male Rage...And second, and probably ultimately more important, the Hour of Angry White Male Rage is far from passing out of our politics.
—Charles P. Pierce, Esquire

Mediocre White Man Falls Apart and Is Promptly Put Back Together...Kavanaugh's absolute master class in white-male privilege....Kavanaugh's alternately blundering, messy, enraged, arrogant performance gave us a close-up look at what white fragility and entitlement look like: Even when you're accused of a serious crime, you're the one who's being persecuted.
—Heather Havrilesky, The Cut

Kavanaugh Borrows From Trump's Playbook on White Male Anger
—Jeremy W. Peters and Susan Chira, The New York Times

Brett Kavanaugh and the Innocence of White Jocks....The privilege, more specifically, pertains to white men, whose

accomplishments we are to take as earned, the result of
grit rather than natural gifts.
—*Lauren Collins, The New Yorker*

To his immense credit, the normally somnolent closeted homosexual Lindsey Graham noted the unhinged white-bashing:

I'm a single white male from South Carolina, and I'm told
I should just shut up, but I will not shut up.

For his part, Kavanaugh said the weeklong National Rape Crisis had nothing to with being white and everything to do with the fact that the Democrats are seeking blood vengeance for his aggressive probing of President Bill Clinton for being a serial perv.

Back when Judge Clarence Thomas—a black dude—was being grilled by Congress about whether he did or didn't harass a black woman named Anita Hill by making tacky office chitchat about Long Dong Silver porn videos, I don't remember the press making race an issue. It was Thomas himself who made it an issue:

From my standpoint, as a black American, as far as I'm
concerned, it is a high-tech lynching for uppity blacks who
in any way deign to think for themselves.

I doubt that Democrats went after Thomas for being black. I sense they went after him for being a black *Republican*.

But since the press seems so keen to harp on the idea of white male rapists, I feel compelled to note that according to government statistics, white males have a lot of catching up to do with other races when it comes to the sordid art of sexual assault. And if interracial rape were the Kentucky Derby, these sad white steeds have barely left the starting gate.

41

Hunting the Domestic Polar Bear

Why has the American media suddenly snapped out of a self-induced coma to pay attention to the Knockout Game? Gullible journos are acting as if it's a spanking-new phenomenon that is sweeping the country, but the practice of black wolf packs cold-cocking pedestrians for cheap thrills has been going on for years. The only thing that's sweeping the country is the media's sudden willingness to talk about it. And not only are they talking, they've also dropped dog whistles such as "youths" and "teens" and are openly noting the assailants' and victims' race. What was the tipping point?

Some will quibble whether it's actually a "game" or a "ritual"—they say calling it a "game" trivializes something that has led to several deaths—but it basically involves walking up to an unsuspecting individual and punching them hard enough to knock them unconscious. You've won the "game" if you knock out your target. Although typically only one member of a group throws the knockout punch—or they take turns until one of them sends the victim to sleep on a concrete bed—this game is almost always performed by packs of black males apparently seeking to impress one another. Whichever lucky individual delivers the knockout blow wins the crown of "Knockout King." Robbery is hardly ever a motive. It appears to be done for fun, to establish ingroup status, and to send a clear message about who rules the streets. Throughout history, those who rule the streets have often served as the shock troops and enforcers for those who rule the nation. This isn't some empty nihilistic ritual—it's a highly political act of establishing dominance and marking one's territory.

Mobs who prey upon the weak are nothing new, although the fact that it's black mobs preying almost exclusively on non-blacks is a fairly recent historical wrinkle. Over the years, the more specific practice of sucker-punching an 80-year-old man to impress your 15-year-old friends has been called "One-Hitter Quitter," "Catch and Wreck," and "Point-em-out, Knock-em-out."

In Illinois a spate of such attacks from around 2008-2010 was known among perps as "Polar Bear

Hunting," most likely because the victims were targeted for being white.

The Midwest appears to be America's most fertile ground for the Knockout Game. In Columbia, MO, parking-lot surveillance video from 2009 shows a group of black attackers approaching a young white male and one of them creeping up from behind to fell him with one blow. The victim suffered whiplash, internal bleeding, and bruising of the brain.

In St. Louis, the game is more commonly referred to as "Knockout King," with attacks going back as far as 2006. One judge allegedly claimed that a single individual was responsible for an estimated 300 such attacks. There was an infamous 2011 incident where the city's mayor pulled up to the scene of a game of Knockout King as it was unfolding.

In April of 2011 a 72-year-old Vietnamese man in St. Louis was sucker-punched by a black male teen and fell to the ground, fatally cracking his head.

In 2012 it proved fatal for a 20-year-old white college student in Minnesota and a 62-year-old Hispanic man in Chicago. In 2013 it claimed the lives of a 72-year-old white man in Syracuse, NY and a 46-year-old homeless Hispanic man in New Jersey.

There have been reports of Knockout Game attacks in Pittsburgh, Philadelphia, and as far away as London, where video captured one punch flattening a 16-year-old girl. And in 2013, perhaps in homage to the fact that the game was gaining national attention, there were six such attacks in New Haven, CT over a two-day period. A 2013 attack in San Diego may herald the Knockout Game's arrival on the West Coast.

The "experts," of course, are expertly clueless. Psychology professor Paul Boxer of Rutgers University calls the perps "impressionable kids" who are running around punching people dead "not because they are hoping to hurt somebody, [but] it's more about risk taking, and new, different and exciting ways of getting into trouble." Dr. Joel Fein of the Philadelphia Collaborative Violence Prevention Center speaks with near-reverence of the "significant inner rage a lot of these children are expressing." A spokesman for the John Jay College of Criminal Justice's Research and Evaluation Center suggests that despite what your eyes tell you, it would be a mistake to see this phenomenon "through the lens of race" and that anyone who views the phenomenon thusly is expressing their own misguided fears and inadequacies. "The root of this Knockout Game," opines James Clark of Better Family Life in St. Louis, "is the lack of recreational opportunities and neighborhood-based programs for our young people."

Even little Phoebe Connolly in Washington, DC, who was punched by a black teen that came up to her and said "KA-POW!" before bloodying her nose as his friends laughed, says it only demonstrates "why we need to better support our youth with activities and youth programs...it's great to see teenagers do incredible things when they're supported and empowered."

Seems to me as if they're plenty empowered. Hell, they might suffer from a *surfeit* of empowerment.

Even Al Sharpton isn't as blind as these white enablers and ethnomasochists. He calls the Knockout Game "insane thuggery" and concedes that "We would not be silent if it was the other way around." Black Atlanta radio host T. J. Sotomayor recorded a 16-minute video where he says white people should counter the Knockout Game with one called the Shootout Game.

But it seems this only became a national story when Jewish leaders spoke up and demanded action after a string of attacks in Brooklyn that targeted multiple Jewish victims. In some cases the victims were Hasidim and thus obviously Jewish, but in others, such as the attack on a 78-year-old woman, it strains belief to think that roving packs of dumb-as-a-stump black teens looking for blood would be able to tell a 78-year-old Jewess from a 78-year-old *shiksa*. The attackers may not have been able to distinguish one light-skinned person from another. We may all look the same to them—pale, easy targets.

New York State Assemblyman Dov Hikind, Rabbi Yaacov Behrman of the Jewish Future Alliance, and Evan Bernstein of the ADL sprung into action, petitioning everyone from NYC's Police Commissioner to President Obama to what I will gently suggest is a sympathetic media to publicize and rectify this horrifying trend that had Brooklyn's Jewish community on edge. In no time at all, an alleged assailant was being charged with a hate crime. These scrappy Tribesmen may not have fought back with their fists, but they used every other available blunt instrument to finally make this a national story. Non-Jewish whites could learn a lesson from such tenacious group solidarity.

Failing that, they could take a tip from the unnamed 40-year-old white man in Michigan who turned the tables on 17-year-old Marvell Weaver and planted two .40-caliber bullets in his ass. Street animals are less likely to pounce on those who haven't been entirely tamed. But any strategy, whether pursued in the courts or on the streets, would be better than taking it on the chin.

42

What if Those Bikers Had Been, Like, Another Color?

Only in America can the media take a deadly shootout among white and Hispanic bikers and somehow make it all about black people. And only in America can these same media megaphone-mouths complain about "the media" without realizing that for all intents and purposes, they *are* the media.

That's exactly what happened in the idiotic editorial aftermath of the May 17, 2015 lunch-hour shootout between rival biker gangs at a Hooters knockoff "breastaurant" called Twin Peaks in south Waco, TX.

Details remain sketchy about the incident and, as is typically the case with such violently chaotic events, eyewitness testimonials wildly contradict one another. What is known is that nine people died. All of them were reportedly bikers, and all but one or two of them appear to have been members of the Cossacks motorcycle gang.

At least one victim was a member of the larger and better-organized Bandidos gang. His name was Manuel Isaac Rodriguez, so I'll go out on a limb here and guess that like George Zimmerman, he was one of those "white Hispanics." The only shooting fatality that was allegedly "unaffiliated" with an organized biker gang was Jesus Delgado Rodriguez—again, I'll presume he was a "white Hispanic."

What's intensely unclear at the moment is exactly who did most of the killing. Some biker-friendly witnesses claim that cops killed every last biker. Other estimates lowball it, asserting that police killed four out of the nine victims.

That's right—even by a low estimate, cops killed four presumably white gang members. And yet no whites rioted. To my knowledge, the last group of reckless arsonists who tried to burn Waco down was the ATF in 1993.

This time around, police swiftly quashed the violence and promptly arrested 172 bikers and biker associates who'd been at the restaurant during the

shootout, charging them all with criminal conspiracy and setting each individual's bail at a steep $1
million. In short, police showed a much more
aggressive response to this incident—which
couldn't have lasted more than five minutes—than
they did to prolonged rioting in Ferguson and Baltimore. But if you were merely to note this fact,
you would be deviating from The Script and told to
shut your filthy bigoted piehole.

One site shows mug shots of 153 arrestees; of these,
a full 42 of the police descriptions classify the
accused as "Hispanic" rather than white. Since the
Cossacks are affiliated with the whites-only Hells
Angels and the Bandidos have always been open
to Hispanic membership—even their logo depicts
a gun-and-machete-wielding male in a som-
brero—it's probably not entirely insane to assume
that most of the Hispanic arrestees were affiliated
with the Bandidos. It might not even be completely
cuckoo to wonder whether a subtext of this ongoing Cossacks/Bandidos rivalry has something to do
with white/Hispanic ethnic tension.

According to the FBI, the Bandidos are affiliated
with the Mexican drug cartel Los Zetas, so they are
apparently much more Hispanic-friendly that many
in the media would allow. The sputtering scribes
who complained about how "the media" handled
this incident framed it mostly as an example of ram-

pant white-on-white violence which, as everyone knows, "the media" downplays because "the media" clearly hates black people. A saner argument would be that since the media all but ignored the Hispanics in this equation, the media hates Hispanic people and loves blacks. But the media will call you insane for trying to make that argument.

Much was made of a photo depicting white bikers calmly assembled under the supervision of a gunwielding cop. The inference we were instructed to draw from this photo is that cops enjoy wearing riot armor and spraying innocent black protestors with tear gas, while they treat murderous white criminals with kid gloves. An alternate inference one could draw from this photo is that white arrestees are less likely to resist arrest than newly canonized black criminal-saints such as Mike Brown, Eric Garner, and Freddie Gray. But that would be racist, so sweep all traces of that thought from your mind.

There was also wailing and gnashing of teeth over the fact that "the media" didn't make a big stink about the "root causes"—such as poverty and single-mother families—of such lawlessness. Again, this was trotted out as evidence that the media is racist against black people, rather than the more likely explanation, which is that the media is constantly making *excuses* for black people.

And, but of course, there was loud and innumerate screaming about how America only focuses on black criminality, making it seem as if blacks are, you know, disproportionately represented in criminal behavior or something, which everyone already knows is a completely nutty idea.

Earl Ofari Hutchinson—he's black, in case the "Ofari" didn't tip you off—wrote that media coverage of the event unveils "a grotesque truth about American hypocrisy" that has "reared its ugly head again." Sally Kohn of CNN wailed that "When white people commit violent acts, they are treated as aberrations, slips described with adjectives that show they are unusual and in no way representative of the broader racial group to which they belong." Throwing all facts to the wind, a black male writer for Salon who calls himself Mensah Demary claims that the event featured 100 bikers shooting at one another—according to all accounts it was only a handful at best—and that white bikers are afforded a "privilege of individuality" that is denied to black thugs.

Are any of these accusations remotely related to reality in any known universe? Of course not! Why would you even ask such a silly question?

Let's look at the thing that scares leftist race-baiters the most: numbers. The word "white" is often statistically muddied by Hispanics who identify as white, but a conservative estimate is that whites outnumber blacks in America by a quotient of five to one. Yet blacks account for around 31% of American gang membership, while whites comprise a mere 13%. Considering that blacks are outnumbered by five to one, a black male is thus twelve times more likely than a white male to be a gang member. (Demographically, the rulers of the roost are Hispanic Americans, who comprise around half of all American gang members.)

The combined estimated American membership of the Bandidos and their chief rivals, the Hells Angels, is less than two thousand. According to the FBI's 2013 National Gang Report, street gangs outnumber biker gangs by a factor of around 35-1. In Chicago alone, the Latin Kings street gang numbers around 25,000. The combined gang membership of Chicago and Los Angeles is around a quarter million. There are thought to be over one million gang members currently in America. So, numerically at least, a couple thousand bikers aren't much of a problem.

When the gunpowder had settled outside the Twin Peaks restaurant in Waco, there were nine corpses. But in 2012 alone, there were an estimated 2,363 gang homicides nationwide. The raging majority of these had nothing to do with white people, whether as killers or victims. Compared to overall gang deaths yearly, the bloodbath in Waco was indeed an aberration rather than business as usual.

But you wouldn't know that from listening to the media. They insist you ignore the numbers and see what happened in Waco as part of a much larger problem—one that's conveniently impossible to solve because it doesn't even exist.

43

A Racial Fort Sumter?

In June 2015, nine black men and women were shot to death at Emanuel AME Church in Charleston, SC. As the young white male shooter was picking off his victims, he reportedly told them that blacks "had to go" because they were taking over the country and raping white women.

Anyone else get a sense that this is only the beginning of something huge and that it won't end well?

The church sits only a half-mile from Fort Sumter, where gunshots started the Civil War.

According to officials, accused killer Dylann Roof, 21, confessed to them that the purpose of his attack was to start a race war. A friend also told ABC News that Roof had spoken of his desire to single-handedly spark a race war.

Finally—after years of what seemed like an endless string of hate-crime hoaxes and other overblown cases where a fabricated or trumped-up white-on-black race-hate angle turned out to be dubious or nonexistent—America appears to have a genuine, bona fide white-on-black mass murder inspired by racial hatred on its hands.

This incident might be the one that, as the blacks are fond of saying, takes it to that other level.

This is not a Tawana Brawley or a Trayvon Martin or a Duke Lacrosse or a Mike Brown situation. As the story takes shape, this appears to be some blank-faced white loner with a Moe Howard haircut who reputedly pecked out an online manifesto clearly articulating his disdain for blacks and Jews and why he felt the need to kill them.

All the people who've been howling for years that America is a place where "black bodies" are routinely brutalized by whites finally have a case that possibly exceeds even their wildest dreams. I'll bet some of them are pleased as punch.

In addition to claiming that Roof confessed to the murders, authorities confirmed that he was the owner of a website called Last Rhodesian, which failed to load every time I tried accessing it over the weekend, presumably because it was being bombarded with requests in the wake of Roof's massacre.

Pictures on the site purportedly show the glum, sullen, and not-all-there-in-the-head young accused race-killer wearing patches of the Rhodesian flag and the flag of South Africa during apartheid. He is also shown hoisting a Confederate flag, burning an American flag, and posing on a beach in front of a giant 1488 he'd presumably etched in the sand. It also shows him pointing a .45-caliber pistol at the camera, which is presumably the gun he allegedly used in Wednesday night's killing spree.

Really, you couldn't have scripted it better—assuming it wasn't scripted.

The site also contains a 2,500-word essay that ends with an apology for any typos, perhaps making it the only killer's manifesto in world history where the killer was at least considerate enough to care about grammar.

In the essay, Roof claims that the Trayvon Martin case "truly awakened me....How could the news be blowing up the Trayvon Martin case while hundreds of these black on White murders got ignored"? He avers that "Niggers are stupid and violent," whites are "in fact superior," and that

America's modern racial problems are due to "Jewish agitation of the black race." He says that he considers Jews to be white, but that their "identity" is what leads to trouble. He suggests finding a way to "turn every Jew blue for 24 hours," which would lead to a "mass awakening."

And then comes what is essentially his declaration of war:

> I have no choice. I am not in the position to, alone, go into the ghetto and fight.

> I chose Charleston because it is [the] most historic city in my state, and at one time had the highest ratio of blacks to Whites in the country.

> We have no skinheads, no real KKK, no one doing anything but talking on the internet. Well someone has to have the bravery to take it to the real world, and I guess that has to be me.

Well, OK then. I suppose one can't fault him for not walking the walk.

When I heard about Dylann Roof's spree, I thought of 2010's Hartford Distributors shooting, wherein Omar Thornton, a black former employee of a beer distribution company, shot eight white former coworkers to death before killing himself. Thornton's white girlfriend would claim that he'd been taunted with racial epithets while at work, although even the nonwhite employees at the company denied that any such events ever occurred.

As with the Charleston shooting, racial animus appeared to be a motivating factor for Thornton. The main difference is that you've likely never heard of Omar Thornton, while you are already painfully aware of Dylann Roof.

That is no coincidence. I'd even suggest it's by design.

I suspect the double standard exists to simultaneously whip up black rage and white resentment. As it is currently configured, our media/government complex focuses almost exclusively on anti-black horror stories—whether real or imagined—while it outright ignores or buries stories about black-on-white violence.

This creates unnecessary resentment on both sides. Blacks get the false impression that they're being disproportionately murdered by whites—rather than, you know, other blacks. And many whites who've been victimized by black violence feel that either no one believes them, no one cares about them, or that everyone feels that they deserved it anyway because of, you know, history and stuff.

How is that anything but a divisive strategy? How can either side win a game with rules like that?

"We don't need any more bloodshed and we don't need a race war," black activist J. Denise Cromwell told a reporter. "Charleston has a lot of racial tension....We're drowning and someone is pouring water over us."

A white friend messaged me with much the same sentiment:

> Situations like Ferguson, Baltimore, Charleston, etc. are manipulated and exploited to support a narrative. A narrative, that for all intents and purposes, would have had the Manson Family jizzing in their bell-bottomed pants in delight. I'm leery as hell. We're all getting played against each other. We're the starving tigers at a Chinese zoo being taunted with meat in the hopes that we'll fight.

I, too, have the queasy sense that strings are being pulled and that we're being lured into a war that's being set up to happen whether we like it or not.

44

Some Dead Bodies Are More Equal Than Others

The Confederate battle flag was taken down in July 2015 outside South Carolina's Statehouse, and barring another Civil War, it is never going up again.

This extensively publicized event was egged on by South Carolina's nonwhite governess and greeted with high holy hosannas from those who haughtily claim to be on the right side of history. Down to their quivering livers, the general public understood that this sweepingly symbolic act was immediate retribution for the nine black churchgoers who were shot dead in Charleston, SC by a scrawny white loner with a bowl cut and a Rebel flag fetish. For those who hate all things Southern and white, this was a joyously orgasmic culmination topping off weeks of nonstop anti-Confederate hysteria.

Examples of such chest-pounding moral panicking included major corporate vendors banning the further sale of Confederate memorabilia, the City of Memphis voting to exhume Nathan Bedford Forrest's corpse, the *Dukes of Hazzard* being pulled from TV syndication, and even calls to ban *Gone With the Wind*, which for most of my youth was the American public's consensus choice for the greatest movie ever made.

All these broad-brush acts of historical erasure were intended to commemorate nine dead in Charleston—a tally which is, oh, only about 4,500 short of how many blacks kill one another every year in America.

Lost in the shuffle were the 300,000 or so white Southern males who died fighting under that Rebel flag. Their lives ceased to matter entirely.

Three hundred thousand corpses are *staggeringly* more than the nine who died in Charleston or the 3,445 American blacks who were lynched between 1882 and 1968. (And no one seems to mention the 1,297 whites that were lynched during that same period, most likely because they weren't even aware of them.) Nor does that total include the fifty-thousand-plus Southern civilians who died as a direct result of that bloody conflict.

Every third Southern household lost a family member in the Civil War. And the overwhelming majority of white Southern households did not own a single slave. And *still* they're not allowed to mourn their dead ancestors?

In order to serve a narrative dictated by the new status quo, the nine dead black churchgoers' lives must be deemed far more important than the 300,000 dead Southern peckerwoods from the Civil War. That's a swap of about 33,000 dead peckerwoods for every dead black Charleston churchgoer. Not a bad deal at all—at least if you aren't a peckerwood.

One group's suffering is being enshrined and sanctified, while the other group's suffering is dismissed and erased. One group's suffering is being honored at the other group's expense. One group's history is openly being shat upon to help enable the other group to feel good about its own less-than-glorious past. It's almost like a postmortem "three-fifths rule," but in this case, it's more like a *zero*-fifths rule. Those dead Confederate bodies stop counting at all. Suddenly, through the magic of progressive algebra, 300,000 becomes zero.

Your history means nothing. Your history lost to our history. You are on the wrong side of history, and we are on the winning side of destiny. So shut up and get with the program, or we will roll right over your burial plot without planting daisies. Basically, they're telling them what white settlers told the Injuns way back when. And what's bitterly amusing is that they're too blinded by their own toxic moralism to see it.

Even though many of them have never so much as placed one pinkie toe south of the Mason-Dixon Line, they will dictate to Southerners exactly what that flag meant and precisely how guilty they should feel about it. And they'll refuse to see anything arrogant or bossy or triumphalist about it. And they will definitely fail to see how their moral disgust and sneering condescension isn't all that different from how slaveowners acted toward those over whom they wielded power through superior force.

For the same reason—because the losers don't write the story—you're hardly ever reminded of the 50 million or so non-Jewish civilians who perished in WWII or the 100-plus million who died under communism. Their dead bodies aren't nearly as important because *their minds weren't right.* The idea persists that Southern whites and German citizens *deserved* to get killed because their little black hearts harbored unpardonable sentiments. Because of their *beliefs* they weren't truly human, so all those bodies stacked up to the sun like pancakes are more like wildlife management than murder.

They tell unreconstructed Southerners to quit whining and shut the hell up about their Lost Cause, but they'd never dare say the same thing to a so-called Native American.

"But that war was so long ago." Yeah, so was slavery.

If all of America's wealth and power had been built on black slavery, the South would have *easily* won the war. Instead, they were outmanned, outgunned, and outspent. The Union didn't win because their cause was more righteous—they won because they had the guns and the money and the human cannon fodder to spare.

You never hear of Union soldiers raping slave women or of the North economically raping the South for at least a century after the war ended. You won't hear about how the vengeful angels of Reconstruction rained down holy hell upon average Southern whites.

In their effort to enshrine and sanctify one group's history, they feel compelled to dismiss and erase another group's history—all in the delusional, quixotic quest to enforce some dim notion of "tolerance" that serves as a convenient mask to cloak a naked drive for power.

It is precisely those who insist that all living humans are equal who also insist that not all dead bodies should be counted equally. They talk about leveling the playing field, but never about leveling the graveyard.

In order to properly remember those nine, we must wipe away all traces of those 300,000. The message is coming through as loud as a Rebel yell: White Southern lives don't matter.

So much of history is about who gets forgotten in the retelling. The winners not only get to write the history books—they get to keep rewriting them until the losers cease to exist. Just like war, history is a zero-sum game. You either write it, or you get written out of it.

45

The Suspect Said He Wanted to Kill White People

America's modern race-obsessed progressive media exhibits symptoms of brainwashing that are so severe, they make North Korea look positively libertarian.

To hear them tell it, in July 2016 a black man in Minnesota "was shot dead for a broken taillight" a mere day after a black man in Louisiana "was shot dead for selling CDs." *Mais pourquoi?* Because, dummy, of "our nation's carnal desires to spill black blood." Duh! What are you—some kind of racist or something?

I often marvel at the magical mystical soothsaying ability of self-proclaimed reporters who were likely hundreds if not thousands of miles from the crime scene yet are able to now not only precisely *what* happened, but also exactly *why* it happened.

The *Daily Mail* reported that in both cases, the victims "were shot by white police officers." The Huffington Post said that the victim in Louisiana was "unarmed."

In a nation already well beyond Race Crazy, this news, however nonfactual it may have turned out to be, did not bode well.

In July 2016 during a Black Lives Matter "peaceful protest" in Dallas, a black Army vet who was obviously sympathetic to BLM's cause decided to "protest" by shooting five police officers dead as well as injuring seven other cops and two civilians.

As our countless friendly Negro readers are fond of saying, shit just got real.

Democratic politicians did not wait for the blood to dry before definitively stating that the two police shootings of black victims were racially motivated. But they didn't say anything about the Dallas massacre being racially motivated.

Regarding the shooting death of Philando Castile in Falcon Heights, MN, Governor Mark Dayton verbally ejaculated thusly:

Would this had happened if those passengers were white?
I don't think it would've. So I'm forced to confront, and I
think all of us in Minnesota are forced to confront, [that]
this kind of racism exists.

Regarding the shooting death of Alton Sterling in
Baton Rouge, LA, Hillary Clinton leaped to politically expedient conclusions and belched the following thought-queefs from her twat:

Something is profoundly wrong when so many Americans
have reason to believe that our country doesn't consider
them as precious as others because of the color of their
skin.

Barack "Blowfly" Obama flaulated thusly from his
mouth:

When incidents like this occur, there's a big chunk of our
citizenry that feels as if, because of the color of their skin,
they are not being treated the same....This is not just a
black issue, not just a Hispanic issue. This is an American
issue that we all should care about.

"This is not just a black issue?" Apart from the fact
that the two shooting victims were black, where's
the proof that it's a black issue at all?

Hi-yella seventh-degree-black-belt wigger Shaun
King of the *New York Daily News*, never a man who
seemed very fond of reality, claims that:

Extrajudicial deaths of men, women and children at the hands of police have never been this widespread in the history of America.

Is that true? Of course not! Fatal police shootings of black men in the USA are down from around 100 a year in the 1960s to about 35 yearly these days. Taking into account the fact that America's black population has roughly doubled in that timespan, on a per-capita basis, police shootings of black men have plummeted around 80% since the 1960s.

Kindly allow me to spotlight some of the details of what happened in these cases that may have escaped your attention.

Despite being described by friends and loved ones as a "sweet person" and a "respected man," Louisiana's Alton Sterling was a convicted pedophile. He'd also been previously arrested for public intimidation, aggravated battery, possession of a stolen firearm, burglary, and, ominously, resisting arrest. Contrary to some reports, police did not confront him for selling CDs, but because a homeless man had called 911 to report that someone matching Sterling's description had threatened him with a gun outside a convenience store. A pair of white cops originally Tasered him and wrestled him to the ground as Sterling continued to struggle. One officer fell under the impression that the suspect was reaching for a gun, whereupon he shot Sterling dead in the chest. Immediately after the shooting, an officer reached into Sterling's back pocket and removed a gun. Graphic video footage of the shooting confirms all this.

Despite being described by associates as "one of the softest-spoken people you've ever met" and "a very even-keeled man" who had "a cheerful disposition," Minnesota's Orlando Castile apparently identified as a Crips gang member who in 2011 wished his Twitter followers a "Merry CRIPmas and happy BLUE year !!!!!"

He also fit the description of an armed robber who'd pulled off a heist at a Super USA Convenience Store four days before and about four blocks away from where a Hispanic—*not* white—cop named Jeronimo Yanez would shoot him dead. Despite initial reports that police had stopped—and killed—him over a broken taillight, video taken after the shooting shows that both of his taillights were working just fine. And according to a police scanner recording, Officer Yanez told the dispatcher:

> *I'm going to stop a car. I'm going to check IDs. I have reason to pull it over....The two occupants just look like people that were involved in a robbery....The driver looks more like one of our suspects, just 'cause of the wide set nose.*

Well, whaddaya know? The only reason that skin color comes into the picture is because the driver fit the description of a black man who'd pulled off a nearby robbery only days earlier.

Also conveniently clipped out of many media accounts is the fact that Castile was carrying a gun and reportedly told the officer as much. His alleged girlfriend Diamond Reynolds began livestreaming the festivities on Facebook shortly after Castile was shot and the life was bleeding out of him. She claims that immediately after Castile told Yanez that he had a gun and that Reynolds added that he had a permit for it, Yanez shot him to death.

But according to Yanez's lawyer, "The shooting had nothing to do with race and everything to do with the presence of that gun," adding Yanez is Latino and, therefore, I guess, not capable of racial hatred.

But despite all these mitigating details, the firm media narrative remained that the back-to-back shootings were yet another sign that white devil cops enjoy gargling the blood of African innocents. So while Black Lives Matter nimrods were having a "peaceful protest" in Dallas mere blocks from where JFK was killed by a sniper, a 25-year-old black sniper named Micah Xavier Johnson murdered five white cops. He then had an hours-long standoff with police before they blew him up with a robot-delivered bomb.

Dallas Police Chief David Brown—a black man—says that during the standoff,

> *The suspect said he was upset at white people. The suspect said he wanted to kill white people, especially white officers.*

For all anyone knows, the Hispanic cop in Minnesota and the two white cops in Louisiana shot their victims because they were afraid that their armed victims would shoot them first. But here's a case where the shooter comes right out and states his motive—he wanted to kill white people. But what is the media narrative? White racism caused all this. Of *course* it did. White racism also caused subsequent copycat shootings of cops in Tennessee, Texas, Missouri, and Georgia. How else would you explain the specter of black people saying they want to kill white people—and then doing it—other than blaming the white people who made the black people want to do it?

Hello, Black America. My name is Jim. I'm going to delicately suggest that if you don't want to be constantly encountering police, it would behoove you to cease committing crime at such astronomical levels.

And if black lives matter to you as much as you claim they do, maybe focus on the 5,000 or so black-on-black murders you commit yearly at least as much as you obsess over the three dozen or so black men killed by white cops every year. And, what the hell, just a suggestion here—quit burning your cities to the ground every time a black man dies at the hands of police. What was the end result of you torching Baltimore over the death of Freddie Gray? Your city saw 344 murders in 2015 compared to 217 the year before. It's probably safe to assume that 100 of those additional murder victims were black. So to show your solidarity and bravery and support of black lives, you torch your city over one dead black guy, scare the police away, and then murder an extra hundred black guys.

Doesn't that seem dumb to you?

You've razed black neighborhoods to the ground all over America by making holy martyrs out of incurable fuckups from Rodney King onward. Once the facts pour in, every Trayvon Martin and Michael Brown and Eric Garner—and now Alton Sterling and Philando Castile—winds up to be far sleazier and much less innocent than originally depicted.

All I'm saying, Black America, is that you need better heroes than these. I know you can do it. Don't let me down.

46

Blacks Rape Preteen Hispanic in Texas, Whites Get Blamed

Over one cruelly protracted evening in November 2010 in the tiny Texas town of Cleveland—up in the ragged piney woods fifty miles northeast of the giant flying-cockroach terrarium called Houston—an 11-year-old girl was passed around like a meaty pre-pube rag doll between two dozen or so males ranging in age from 14 to 26.

Police have made eighteen arrests in an ongoing investigation. So far, all of those charged are black, and the preteen victim has been identified as Hispanic. A judge has placed a gag order on the case, presumably to throw a wet blanket over what is rapidly becoming an ethnic tinderbox in this town of 8,000 where the major employers are Walmart and a prison.

Cell phones and text-messaging made this Super Preteen Gangbang a technologically orchestrated sex crime—call it a Flash Rape. Court documents say the 11-year-old victim initially accepted an offer from a 19-year-old male with prior drug convictions to go "riding around" with him and two other males on November 28. They wound up at one of the male's houses, where the girl was threatened with a beating if she refused to strip naked and service them. She complied, and as she was being passed around like a Sex Bong from the bathroom to the bedroom, four other males were invited via cell phone to come ride the train. They soon arrived, but when one of the attacker's aunts unexpectedly returned home, the entire crew, including the naked 11-year-old, escaped out a back window.

They resumed activities at a trash-covered, glass-strewn trailer home that had been abandoned since Hurricane Ike rendered it uninhabitable in 2008. As phone calls and text messages were beamed out through the black neighborhood known as "The Quarters" and the number of assailants swelled from the initial trio to as many as 28, at least one of them thought it'd be a smart idea to immortalize the festivities on video. According to an affidavit, the victim "stated that digital still images and digital video images of the sex acts were recorded by one or more individuals using cellular telephones." One of these DIY documentarians also thought it wise to later share the kiddie porn with several other Cleveland High School students. His video spread like scrotal warts from one cell phone to the next, causing one student to tell a teacher, who told the police, who launched an investigation.

Police began making arrests of teenaged and adult men with names such as Cedric DeRay Scott, Kelvin Rashad King, Jamarcus Norris Napper, and Devo Shaun Green. Every mugshot and series of mugshots revealed the perps to be exclusively derived from Cleveland's black population. One of the accused had been free on bond but is still facing charges for a 2008 shooting death. Another had been facing felony beefs for two aggravated robberies over the past year, one regarding a gun to the head and the other involving full-blown gunplay. Yet another had served a month in jail the previous year for assaulting a family member.

Local blacks instinctively defended the defendants and got way down low with the art of blaming the victim. The 11-year-old who'd been used as a sexual pincushion and is probably emotionally destroyed for life was called both a "snitch" and a "willing participant" who "dressed older than her age, wearing make-up." Women made comments such as "She lied about her age. Them boys didn't rape her. She wanted this to happen" and "Where were [the parents] when this girl was seen wandering at all hours with no supervision and pretending to be much older?" James D. Evans III, black defense attorney for several of the defendants, said "the victim was seeking attention and she wants to be a porn star." One of the accused's mothers appears on video to hoot and holla in a nearly indecipherable Lone Star ghetto twang about how it's the Hispanic parents' fault for supervising her little girl so poorly that she got mega-raped.

It doesn't seem to occur to Ghetto Mom that the same could be said about herself and her accused-rapist son, as well as all the parents of the two dozen or so other perps. But tribal instincts have a way of blotting out obvious facts that might be harmful to the tribe.

The victim was removed from her own family and placed in Child Protective Services after the event. There are rumors that she had a Facebook page where she "makes flamboyant statements about drinking, smoking, and sex" and spoke of "being hurt many times" and how she "let people take advantage" of her. The victim's mother, identified only as "Maria," insists that the perps knew her daughter was only an 11-year-old who "still loves stuffed bears." She says she's received numerous threatening calls and that police have urged her family to relocate rather than face the stitches that the ghetto gives to bitches who are snitches.

While the victim's mother was receiving phoned threats from blacks, local Hispanics allegedly made death threats to a church that planned to host Houston race pimp Quanell X, former crack dealer and current New Black Panther who'd promised to blow into town in defense of the accused. According to Mr. X, police had told him to cancel the church meeting to avoid exacerbating "racial unrest between black and Hispanic groups."

Quanell and his Quan'tourage relocated their event to a community building. Rubbing salt and squeezing lemon juice in Latino flesh wounds, Quanell conceded that local Hispanics had "a right to be angry with black men who ravaged a young girl...but the first house you need to stop at is her Mama and Daddy's house!," a statement which was cheered and amen'd by what looked like an entirely black audience. Although he claimed he "did not come here this evening to jump on an 11-year-old girl," he also questioned why she "didn't report the attack to the authorities herself." He wondered out loud why "only young black men had been arrested" for this crime, failing to ponder that perhaps the videotaped evidence only *showed* young black men. Again—those tribal instincts can blind a man, especially one who makes his living as a tribesman.

Mr. X, who had once urged blacks to "mug you some good white folks" and "give these white folks hell from the womb to the tomb," accused the city of Cleveland of practicing "selective prosecution" toward only black males, blamed the town for a pervasive climate of "white racism," and compared police investigators to the KKK.

Of *course* he did. Sooner or later, you *knew* white people were going to be blamed for this, no matter if every cracker in Texas had been vacationing on the moon while these two dozen emotionally and cognitively retarded buzzards eagerly feasted on that preteen Latina's teeny-tiny turkey twat.

Media outlets picked up on this white-racism theme and ran with it like Usain Bolt fleeing a convoy of monster trucks.

On another video, you hear a Houston TV announcer solemnly intone what "Cleveland has a history of racial tension" because "Twenty-two years ago, white police officers were accused of beating an African-American man in prison." What you *don't* hear him say is that all the accused officers in that case were acquitted, meaning if that's the best they can come up with, the town really didn't have much of a history of racial tension until now. ABC News quoted local social worker Brenda Myers saying the gang-rape case was "becoming a black and white issue" that was "seg-regating our community again," though she failed to elucidate why white people were relevant to this case at all.

Finally, unnamed "witnesses" said they saw several white men with shaved heads in a pickup truck shouting "Kill all the niggers!" as they drove in broad daylight down a busy Cleveland street. Par-don me for suggesting that sounds just a touch stereotypical and that the only missing props are Confederate flags, open beer containers, and a shotgun rack. Forgive me also for noting that none of the witnesses, as eager as many of them are to record preteen gang rapes, bothered to record this alleged hate crime. And if you can find it in your heart, absolve me of my sins for daring to comment that at least none of these reputed white men, with their reportedly shaved heads, if they indeed existed, were brick-stupid enough to record them-selves and share the self-incrimination with all their friends.

The American media's bullhorns still blare loudly and continually about dustily ancient interracial-rape sagas: long-buried white rapist slave-masters and generations-old endemic false rape accusations that led to Klan lynchings, the Scottsboro Boys, and Emmett Till. But since white gang rapes of blacks appear to have ceased a long, *long* time ago in America, the modern media eagerly jump like fornicating rabbits on race-rape hoaxes such as Tawana Brawley and the Duke lacrosse case until the truth emerges and everyone hippity-hops away without apologizing—but they remain absolutely 100% mute about modern statistics regarding inter-racial rape in America.

Based on US government stats from 2005, over a third of the verified 111,490 rapes and sexual assaults on white women that year were committed by blacks, leading to a total estimated number of black-on-white victims at 37,460. By contrast, black victims of white sexual predators were listed at 0.0%. Scanning these government stats from 2003 to 2008, I counted 135,207 rapes and sexual assaults perpetrated by blacks against whites and ZERO committed by whites against blacks. For the year 2006, Wikipedia's "Rape in the United States" entry cites statistics that work out to roughly 32,443 black-on-white sexual assaults compared to "a neg-ligible number of white offenders."

Whatever stats you care to scratch over the past generation or two, interracial-rape statistics are similarly lopsided to a degree so absurd, no wonder so many people don't like talking about them. A review of 1988 FBI data by Dr. William Wilbanks revealed "9,406 cases of black-on-white rape and fewer than ten cases of white-on-black rape." A

1974 study in Denver showed that two-fifths of all white rape victims had been raped by blacks but failed to reveal a single instance of a white-on-black rape.

Then again, white people had nothing to do with this incident. They simply got dragged into a situation that was essentially black versus Hispanic. If there's one factoid the mainstream media seems to suppress more than those interracial-rape statistics, it's that people can act racist toward one another without a single white face at the scene of the hate crime.

47

The Night They Punched His Lights Out in Georgia

Shortly before the stroke of midnight on August 24, 2012 in Savannah, GA, a young interracial couple was strolling downtown through a former slave market called Ellis Square. Twenty-three-year-old Andrew Quade, the white boyfriend of a black female named Olufisayo Bakre, would leave in an ambulance after being pummeled unconscious by what Bakre describes as three black males.

"He was basically left for dead," Bakre told a television reporter. "I don't want to go into, like, all the gory details, but, um, they could have stopped, and they kept going....One of them was making racial comments toward us and the other was blowing kisses, so it was very, it was a very aggravating situation to be in."

"I didn't wanna just be like, like, freak out on them, because I thought they were sayin' something to me," Quade told a reporter. "I was just trying to gain, you know, a little more knowledge about the situation, and before we could even do that, there was just, BAM-BAM," said Quade, who may be the same person designated by the same TV station as a "Top Teen" in 2006. Quade reportedly refused to be filmed on camera because his face looked even worse than in gruesome photos that were snapped at the hospital. A full week after the attack, Quade's condition continued to worsen, and he was flown to Atlanta to undergo eye surgery.

"I just hope they get caught, really," Bakre said. "I just hope justice prevails at the end of the day. And this shouldn't happen in this day and age. I know we're in the South and all that yadda-ya, but, I don't know, it's time for a change, I think."

Interesting she should mention the South, a place that is never stereotyped for black-on-white "hate crimes." The South is known as a place where drooling hillbillies rape you and you shouldn't "trust your soul to no backwoods Southern lawyer." It's also where Emmett Till was murdered for allegedly "wolf-whistling" at a white woman.

Then again, Emmett Till was murdered in 1955, while Andrew Quade was beaten unconscious in

2012. But searching their names on Google News—which supposedly documents what's happening now—yielded more than 75 hits for "Emmett Till" for every instance of "Andrew Quade."

Why is that? And why is it considered racist to so much as wonder why? Has all this jibber-jabber about "equality" merely been a power-grabbing wolf in sheep's clothing?

I called the Savannah Police Department's non-emergency line to verify the date that Andrew Quade was assaulted, and a woman who sounded black—kill me for stereotyping—said, "Oh, you mean the hate crime?" But Georgia is one of only five states with no hate-crime law, so it's up to US Attorney General Eric Holder to prosecute the incident under federal hate-crime statutes. Unless you want to die of auto-idiotic asphyxiation, I wouldn't hold my breath.

Living in Georgia, I've heard repeated murmurs that there is no place in the state thicker with racial tension than Savannah. It's presumed that blacks still harbor resentment for the slave era as well as their infamous betrayal near Savannah at the hands of a Union general whose name, in the bitterest of ironies, was Jefferson Davis.

Such resentments have fed upon their own entrails for so long that they linger to this day. Savannah is where racial discrimination is allegedly so rampant, attorneys specialize in filing lawsuits on behalf of the aggrieved. The city now features a monument with an inscription by Maya Angelou about how slaves were forced during the Middle Passage to wallow in one another's "urine and excrement"—a foolproof way to foster racial healing if ever there was one. It's where some people predicted race riots if Georgia went through with its execution of Savannah's convicted cop-killer Troy Davis in 2011. (Davis was executed, but there were no overt riots, only worldwide protests and widespread political pouting.) Early in 2012, the city dealt with what appears to be yet another high-school hate-crime hoax involving an imaginary noose. And Savannah's plump-as-a-pig diabetic celebrity TV chef Paula Deen was recently sued for allegedly using the phrase "bunch of little niggers."

Savannah's City Council, which has recently tilted 5-4 in favor of blacks, reportedly squabbles endlessly along racial lines, egged on by a black mayor who has said things such as "it's our turn" and that he wants a city manager who "looks like me." A local reporter calls Savannah "A diverse and divided city."

But isn't diversity a strength? Isn't it supposed to unite rather than divide? Not if you trace the word's history. According to an online etymology dictionary, the word "diversity" has traditionally meant "disagreement," being "turned different ways," and "being contrary to what is agreeable or right." The word only started acquiring a specifically positive sheen around 1992—coincidentally around the same time that Savannah's population became majority-black. Savannah's mayor now boasts that "majority rule" is "the American way."

But don't expect America's mass media to publicize such triumphalist, race-rooted, turnabout-is-fair-play power-jockeying. And don't expect them to give equal time to racially motivated black-on-white assaults anytime soon. They're too busy hearing imaginary white-racist dog whistles everywhere.

Although America's media mavens created a massively divisive racial issue out of the Trayvon Martin case—a fatal shooting that involved a perpetrator who wasn't exactly white and who apparently was not motivated by racial animosity—they hardly made a peep about the white Buffalo teenager bludgeoned with a brick in 2009 by a group of black males ostensibly because he was dating a black girl. Although the victim in that case claims he was repeatedly racially taunted in the days leading up to a beating that left him slurring his words, the case was not tried as a hate crime. Meanwhile, across the state, a white Brooklyn man was charged with a hate crime after allegedly uttering racial slurs and using a fork to stab a black man who was dining with two white women.

How long will the obvious double standard persist? Exactly as long as everyone keeps their mouths shut for fear of being called bad names. And if you'd rather risk being knocked unconscious than being called a bad name, it's hard to feel any sympathy for you.

48

Kids Make Stupid Decisions

It is with a perverse sort of glee that I can announce we've finally found a violent anti-white attack where the media and law can no longer deny it was motivated by anti-white hatred.

I find it severely depressing that it took a grisly video—which the perps livestreamed on Facebook, for fuck's sake—where four blacks torture an eighteen-year-old schizophrenic bound-and-gagged male while repeatedly taunting him for being white—that finally forced the media and law to grudgingly admit that, *yeah, OK, well, we guess that black people can commit violent "hate crimes" against white people too, goddamnit.*

Oh, they *tried* denying it at first—*hoo-lawdy*, did they try!—but the videotaped evidence was too much to deny. They will proceed to ignore it, just as they've done with thousands of similar attacks over the past few generations, but their boilerplate Narrative of Denial collapsed quickly because to deny what was happening on this video would be to publicly announce to the world that you're a liar, and a bad one at that.

Police claim that on New Year's Eve going into 2017, family members dropped off 18-year-old Austin Hillbourn at a McDonald's in the Chicago suburbs. Hillbourn is white and has allegedly been diagnosed with schizophrenia and attention-deficit disorder. Sometime that night, 18-year-old Jordan Hill—a popular black student at Hillbourn's high school whom relatives say Hillbourn "idolized"—picked him up in a stolen van. Over the next two nights, Hill forced Hillbourn to sleep in the van under freezing Chicago temperatures while Hill visited friends. On Tuesday the pair met up in a West Chicago apartment with 18-year-old Tesfaye Cooper (an aspiring rapper who goes by the handle "PBG HotHead") and the Covington sisters—Brittany (18) and Tanishia (24).

Over the course of what police estimate to be five or six hours, the quartet of blacks forced an obviously terrified Hillbourn to drink water straight from a toilet, bound and gagged him, punched and kicked him, sliced off part of his scalp (and when they noticed blood, one of them joked that "he leakin'!"), put out cigarettes on his head, and repeatedly threatened to murder him—all while laughing their jolly drunken asses off.

During the half-hour or so of the torture that these four numskulls were supremely stupid enough to livestream on Facebook, they make several explicitly racial comments that point to racial hatred as a motive far more than all the recently overhyped Trayvons and Fergusons and Baltimores and Baton Rouges combined—with the stark difference being that white people aren't rioting and burning cities, at least not yet.

In fact, I can't seem to recall evidence of *any* racial motivation in any of those cases, at least as it pertains to recorded statements from the perpetrators. Kindly correct me if I'm wrong. But in this Chicago kidnapping/torture case, the perpetrators mention race over and over and over.

Sample comments uttered by this dusky quartet of blockheads as recorded by their own dumb hands:

> *Fuck Donald Trump, nigga! Fuck white people, boy! Fuck white people, boy!*

> *This nigga right here—he represents Trump.*

> *His ass deserve it. His ass from Europe.*

> *400 years done stopped two years ago.*

If he sit in the sun all day, he will perish. If he sit in the sun all day, he gonna die.

His ass a parasite. He a bug. Literally. He don't belong on this earth.

Goof-ass white man.

The media apologists for such events at Salon and *The New York Times* tried running a deflection move and claimed that if this was indeed a "hate crime"—I HATE that term—it was motivated by a hatred for the disabled rather than a hatred of white people because, well, as you all know, the latter is scientifically impossible. A Chicago police spokesman also claimed that Hillbourn was assaulted due to his "special needs" rather than his race.

But on the video, the term "special needs" isn't mentioned once. The word "white" is mentioned several times.

There was also an initial screaming reluctance to label this a "hate crime," most flagrantly demonstrated in this stultifyingly dumb comment by Chicago Police Department Commander Kevin Duffin during a news conference:

Although they're young adults, they're 18. Kids make stupid decisions. I shouldn't call them kids. They're legally adults, but they're young adults and they make stupid decisions.

Kids make stupid decisions? I think that's what's known in the PR biz as "lowballin' it." This soft-pedaling approach was echoed by CNN's Don Lemon, who blamed the whole sordid affair on "bad home training."

When the backlash to these and similar comments proved to be too strong to keep the narrative afloat, both the media and Chicago authorities succumbed and said it was a "hate crime." All four perps were charged with hate crimes as well as a slew of other criminal offenses. Even the moon-pie-faced squawking choco-harpy Symone Sanders—the former Bernie Sanders campaign spokesnegress who in November said, "Oh, my goodness, poor white people!" when confronted with the fact that video evidence shows in November, a white man in Chicago had been dragged out of a car and beaten by blacks while an onlooker called him "one of them white boy Trump guys"—finally capitulated and said what happened to Austin Hillbourn was a "hate crime."

Apparently panicking in the face of such rapid narrative collapse, the *Chicago Tribune* quickly belched out an article about how, according to FBI statistics, white-on-black "hate crimes" are still more common than the inverse.

But the problem with such stats is a firm cultural and apparently legal reluctance to call *any* black-on-white violence a "hate crime," no matter how strong the evidence is that racial animus was at least partial motivation. Americans know who Dylann Roof is but not Omar Thornton. They remember Rodney King but not Reginald Denny. They're familiar with the murder of Emmett Till—which happened in 1955—but not the much more gruesome murders of Channon Christian and Christopher Newsom, which happened in 2007.

If you remove the very notion of "hate crime" from interracial violence in America and examine the actual stats, an entirely different picture emerges.

According to Department of Justice statistics analyzed by Heather Mac Donald regarding the years 2012 and 2013, blacks are the attackers in 84.9% of violent crimes between blacks and whites. Given differences in population sizes, a black is 27 times more likely to violently attack a white than the inverse.

So I suspect that the very notion of "hate crimes," especially as funneled through an egregious double standard that dictates nonwhites are incapable of even *committing* them, may be a very sneaky and cynical deflection from stark statistical realities about interracial violence.

The videotaped evidence of the Chicago kidnapping/torture reveals beyond a whisper of a doubt that the perps were, if not exactly "kids," extremely stupid. Droolingly stupid. So stupid it seems miraculous that they even knew how to use Facebook for long enough to incriminate themselves. They appear to be possibly even dumber than the bricks that were apparently smashed into their heads and made them this dumb in the first place.

But how dumb was Austin Hillbourn to idolize a black thug who clearly didn't idolize him? How severely naïve was he to get in the stolen van that night? Kids make stupid decisions, and on New Year's Eve at that McDonald's in the Chicago burbs, Austin Hillbourn made the dumbest decision of his life.

Fear has its place. A little bit of fear would have served Austin Hillbourn well. Perhaps his childlike acceptance of someone who wished him harm was part of his mental condition.

But what's clear is that his attackers had no fear. And that may be part of a much bigger problem—the fact that no one seems afraid of white people anymore.

49

Mugging Me Softly

On a Tuesday night in October 2015, I was walking down a poorly lit Brooklyn street en route to meet a friend for dinner when suddenly I noticed a black male strolling alongside me.

He wasn't walking ahead of me or behind me—he was about three feet to my right as if we were best pals and we'd been walking together the whole time. At first I presumed it was a coincidence—that we merely happened to be going the same speed and that within a half-block, one of us would pull ahead of the other and that would be the end of it.

A block later, I tried crossing the street merely to shake him. He stayed glued to my side. After another whole block, I stopped, looked him straight in the eyes, and said, "What's going on here? Why are you following me?"

He stopped along with me. His glazed eyes looked straight into mine. He didn't say a word. He only nodded in the affirmative, even though I hadn't asked him a yes-or-no question.

So I crossed the street again, and he crossed with me, stuck to my side like a Siamese twin. Oh, sorry—a Nigerian twin, maybe?

He was walking alongside me so deliberately that I suspected he was a designated escort leading me into some sort of ambush.

I knew I had suddenly found myself in a potentially dangerous situation, but I wasn't sweating and my heart wasn't pumping any faster. I have this personality quirk where I'm as neurotic as Woody Allen when there's no clear and present danger, but when there's an immediate risk of dying, I'm cold, calm, and calculating.

I kept him in my visual periphery and breathed deeply as I remembered all the joint locks and leg sweeps I'd learned in martial-arts classes. At one point I reached inside my denim jacket to pantomime that I was concealing a gun, then I pulled my hand out quickly when I realized that if he actually was toting a pistol, I might have been signing my death warrant by reaching for a gun that wasn't there.

After more than three blocks of this creepy urban polar bear hunt, I walked up to a pair of young hipstery girls who were closing up shop and locking the doors to their bakery.

"Uh—hi?" I said to them.

My new unwanted friend stopped alongside with me.

"I know this is weird," I continued to the pale-as-bakery-dough girls, "but this guy's been following me for about a half-mile and I don't know what to do here. I asked him what's going on, and he wouldn't even say anything."

One of them looked at my walking companion and asked, "Are you OK, sir?"

He nodded in the affirmative.

"This is weird, right?" I asked the girls, and they nodded in the affirmative.

They asked me whether they should unlock the bakery and allow me to wait inside until he vamoosed. I said he'd probably simply keep waiting, plus I didn't think they should be forced to wait along with me. I also said that I didn't like cops and didn't want to get the cops involved.

At the mention of the word "cops," my pedestrian stalker bolted back in the direction whence we'd come.

I apologized to the girls. "I'm really sorry to have bothered you, but you were the only sign of civilization around here."

When I met my friend for dinner and told him what happened, he speculated that I was being set up for a "soft mugging," which is a term for when homeless people attach themselves to you and won't leave until you give them some money.

Sure, I could have simply hauled off and walloped that guy with a left hook while hoping he didn't have five accomplices waiting in the shadows. But that's easier said than done when you're a white felon with a shaved head and a long history of issuing politically insensitive public statements. So there I was, acutely aware that I could lose my life within the next sixty seconds, fretting about how it would look to the world at large if I got into a street scrap with a black male despite the fact that he'd been actively harassing me.

White male privilege in 2015 means that if I get into any altercation with someone who isn't white or male, I am presumed guilty. It's happened to me with women. And with anti-racist skinheads. And with a black dude who tried breaking into my car. In each case, I was not the instigator, only the one who fought back. But being unapologetically white and male worked *against* me in every case.

Such hard personal experiences lead me to feel that anyone who seriously thinks "white male privilege" exists in 2015 is either a liar or a moron—probably both. The way the deck is stacked these days, being a white male is a disadvantage that hobbles you Harrison Bergeron-style in any dispute with someone who isn't a white male.

When I think of all the taxes that are bled for me in a doomed 'n' dimwitted quest to achieve "social justice" at my expense...and when I ponder that modern media and academia are on an unfettered defamation rampage against all things white and male...it sometimes feels as if all of life is a soft mugging.

50

Biting the Hand That Holds Out the Olive Branch

I've noticed a trend: The more that white people apologize, the more they get mocked. The more they concede, the more that is demanded of them. The more frequently they make gestures of good-will, the more they get emotionally sandblasted with malicious rhetoric about how "whiteness" is a poison that needs to be uprooted and eradicated. And what's bitterly funny is that these well-meaning but fatally clueless Caucasoids can't seem to figure out why this is happening.

The reason is simple: Self-hatred is never attractive, neither individually nor collectively, no matter who's expressing it. It didn't reflect well on blacks when movie clowns such as Mantan Moreland were bugging their eyes out and saying, "Feets don't fail me now!," nor was it appealing when the heavy-lidded Stepin Fetchit played a shuffling, servile black idiot in every appearance.

Yet the default Virtue Mode these days for any white person who doesn't want to be forever banished beyond the Pale—or should that be *into* the Pale?—is to bend over, grab their ankles, wince, and scream, "Pleeze, Massa, don't hurt me!" They are sheltered and stupid enough to see such behavior as a virtue rather than a weakness. They appear to view it as a survival strategy rather than an invitation to murder.

The groups they're trying to appease, though, aren't nearly so naïve. Since people are animals—especially ones who've been encouraged their entire lives to view you as a natural predator who's constantly seeking to kill, maim, defame, and oppress them—they tend to smell blood with every escalating gesture of compassion. It emboldens them to bite the hand that meekly holds out the olive branch.

Of course the clueless white ethnomasochists wind up getting hurt. It's as if they've willingly allowed a giant KICK ME sign to be painted on their backs.

As was seamlessly documented in Howard Bloom's *The Lucifer Principle*, most kings throughout history were overthrown not at the height of their despotism, but after they'd grown soft and started trying to make amends.

They say white people deserve to hate themselves for all the pain and death they've wrought. I say white people are loathsome these days because they're uniquely susceptible to such idiotic guilt-tripping. *That's* the problem with white people—not that it was so easy for them to conquer the world, but that it's so easy to make them feel bad about it.

I sure as hell hate white people these days—they are by far my least favorite racial group—but not because they're innately worth hating. It's because they already hate themselves far too much, and they don't wear it well. I have far more respect for all other groups because *they respect themselves*, whether it's deserved or not.

It's been a long process, but huge swaths of the globe's Caucasian population have been snookered and hoodwinked and bamboozled into thinking that being history's winners should be a matter of shame rather than celebration. You don't see such servile self-abnegation among any other racial group on Earth. Has there been a demographic cluster in world history more thoroughly brain-washed into cheering its own demise than modern white people?

As our culture is currently dictated to us, white ethnomasochism is the only form of ethnic self-hatred that is currently deemed a virtue. Nonwhites are ritually scolded if they *aren't* openly proud of their heritage, whereas whites are publicly reprimanded if they dare to notice anything in white history beyond slavery, colonialism, and the Holocaust.

Look with disgust upon these squirming white worms with their endlessly tacky public displays of self-flagellation, exulting in the idea of their own wickedness, trying to drown their historical sins in a cleansing wave of softly genocidal immigration.

This is the sort of thing that happens in the late stages of a crumbling empire, when the fat, lazy, and pampered have grown so soft they've blinded themselves to the wolf pack waiting at the door that's eager to tear them to pieces.

Believe this—if white people actually held such iron-fisted power and were remotely as ruthless as they are portrayed, there would be no such mocking. People would be scared beyond belief to insult whites, because they'd be forced to deal with drastic consequences—you know, just as any white person these days is publicly destroyed for saying anything remotely unkind about nonwhites.

Truly the most toxic and pervasive form of racial hatred these days is white self-hatred. It's an appallingly ugly phenomenon. A seething loathing for one's group identity, a servile attitude of constant apology for one's very existence, is never attractive.

We are constantly lectured that there was nothing good about the "good old days," that it was one giant charnel house of rape and plunder and exploitation—as if the Third World ever offered *anything* that was either culturally or technologically worth exploiting.

Frank Joyce is a white man who recently pecked out a screed called "White men must be stopped." And Gillian Schutte is a miscegenatin' white South African slag who scribbled one of those endlessly tiresome "Dear White People" open letters to white people from a white person who is ostensibly enlightened enough to see whiteness as a cancer.

They are afflicted with faces that were born, marinated, and sculpted in a culture of relentless white guilt. They are ugly, defeated, self-hating, despicable mugs, the type that would likely enjoy being spat upon. If I were nonwhite, I'd feel entirely justified in walking up to such pathetic visages and saying, "Thanks for your apology—now give me your wallet."

Then take a gander at Hollywood stars John Wayne and Rita Hayworth back when there was no such thing as white guilt—back in the "bad old days" when there was no institutional culture of apology. In fact, look at nearly any white person in photos prior to the 1960s and tell me they don't look more robust, dignified, and full of life than most welfare-siphoning, medication-gobbling, self-loathing, guilt-wracked, demoralized, virtue-signaling white folks these days.

People look better when they're on the attack than when they're in retreat. And that's why most white people don't look very good at all these days.

Nonwhites have a legitimate reason to fear an end of white self-loathing. When white people don't hate themselves, they end up doing something horrible—like ruling the world.

Printed in Great Britain
by Amazon